MY VALUE CREATION JOURNEY

AN AUTOBIOGRAPHY OF MY WORK

BARTLEY J. MADDEN

Hardcover: 979-8-9896739-0-2
Softcover: 979-8-9896739-1-9
eBook: 979-8-9896739-2-6

Editor: Jack Reardon
Copyeditor: Kim Bookless
Cover Design: Alejandro Renteria
Interior Design: Vicky Vaughn Shea, Ponderosa Pine Design
Publishing Strategist: Holly Brady, Brady New Media Publishing

Published by the Bartley J. Madden Foundation, Naples, Florida
Printed in the United States of America

In celebration of my family—

Maricela, Lucinda, Miranda, Jeffrey, Gregory, Peg, Sarah, and Katie.

Contents

Preface and Overview

This book is an autobiography of my work that began with a commitment to understand how business firms create value and how their performance translates to stock market valuations. This is the thread that connects all of my work.

I'm a workaholic. Always was. Always will be. I remember working twenty-plus hours a week in a gas station while attending high school in the late 1950s. As a practical matter, I needed to be financially independent. Working on cars, including my 1932 Ford three-window coupe hot rod, was part of why I chose mechanical engineering as a college major. If you have seen the classic movie *American Graffiti*, the Friday night cruising in my assorted hot rods, as depicted in the movie, was part of my life in Los Angeles (the San Fernando Valley).

Chapter 1 starts with my college days and highlights how boxing became part of my life. After receiving a BS in mechanical engineering, I worked at the Los Angeles Department of Water and Power (see photo on the front cover) for a short period before spending two years in the Army during the Vietnam War. I also discuss a high-risk decision to co-found Callard Madden & Associates in 1970. Starting a firm with savings amounting to one month's rent, no backup source of financial support, and a boatload of student loan debt was high risk. But it profoundly changed my life, as described in chapter 1. Callard Madden enabled me to engage full-time in one of my core passions—better understanding a firm's value-creation process. Call that passion #1.

Passion is what makes capitalism tick: passion to create a uniquely satisfying experience for customers; passion to create new products that scream that the old way is dead. Passion is also needed to make capitalism itself better and to help all of us secure a better future. The purpose of this autobiography is to share my passions with you so that my journey may cause you to more energetically embrace a value-creation way of thinking and living. And live a more satisfying and purposeful life. In addition, value creation is scalable, offering an opportunity for a new political paradigm that cuts across rigid ideologies to the benefit of all.

In studying value creation (and dissipation) by firms, I found myself digging deeper into systems thinking (passion #2) and knowledge building (passion #3). Value creation at the firm level means value creation by individuals, teams, groups, and organizations. And scale-up value creation by firms in the aggregate and we have a window into society's economic progress. This is very cool.

My work career can be categorized as research in finance and in knowledge building. (I never considered these to be separate topics.) Chapter 1 describes my earlier finance work. A critical part of connecting a firm's long-term performance to its stock market valuation is the life-cycle framework. This has proven especially useful and is explained in chapter 1. Actual historical life-cycle track records will be presented in later chapters, which provide a visual history of the economic drivers of value creation or, as the case may be, value dissipation.

Chapter 2 discusses the Knowledge Building Loop. It deconstructs the knowledge-building process into easily understood steps that all business students (and managers) can immediately use. With a better lens to see the world, my approach to value creation provides useful insights on important business/economic issues. Three examples follow in chapters 3, 4, and 5; all are reprints of my open-access journal articles, each demonstrating practical ways of dealing with a variety of tough issues.

Theories are helpful in pinpointing the relevant issues so that we can better see the world and ask better questions. Chapter 3 introduces my Pragmatic Theory of the Firm. Knowledge building is central to this theory. To highlight how the knowledge-building process is effectively used, and how it can be acclimated to any problem, I discuss how the Wright brothers taught the world how to fly—an interesting case study in and of itself.

In 2020, I wrote *Value Creation Principles: The Pragmatic Theory of the Firm Begins with Purpose and Ends with Sustainable Capitalism*. The book's core ideas are laid out in an article that is republished as chapter 4. My theory of the firm offers a logically sound (and much-needed) explanation of why a firm's long-term survival (and prosperity) depends on its knowledge-building proficiency. The theory provides pragmatic insights for boards of directors, management, and long-term investors, and by connecting management's role in creating value to capitalism itself, it deserves to be part of the business school curriculum.

Chapter 5 challenges the conventional thinking that implementation of Environmental, Social, and Governance (ESG) metrics will linearly lead to needed changes in company behavior, eventually resulting in a successful Net Zero transition. A systems view suggests that innovation, not ESG metrics, will be the prime mover in achieving Net Zero.

In chapter 6, I discuss the Madden Center for Value Creation, which is part of the business school at Florida Atlantic University. One of the many creative initiatives started at the Center is the Certificate in Value Creation, a thirty-hour online course. The first cohort attracted fifteen hundred participants from over forty countries. The course consists of seven units that build on chapters in my *Value Creation Principles* and cohesively and meaningfully weave in articles and videos from worldwide experts. The plan is to scale this course worldwide.

Another Madden Center initiative is the Free To Choose Medicine (FTCM) proposal to achieve much-needed FDA reform. Interestingly, it represents a microcosm of my own value-creation journey: promote intellectual tools that yield creative specifications of problems; use a systems-thinking lens to search for obsolete assumptions; and produce value-creation solutions. FTCM could complement the FDA's exorbitantly expensive drug approval system. With FTCM, promising new drugs with demonstrated safety and efficacy in early clinical testing could receive conditional approval. All treatment results and relevant patient data would be recorded in a registry so that doctors and patients could compare approved drugs vs. conditionally approved drugs. Patients, advised by their doctors, could then make informed choices thereby enabling patients to gain early access to potentially life-changing or life-saving medical treatment. This nicely illustrates the usefulness of viewing the overall drugs-to-patients system, of which the FDA is a part, thereby enabling a strikingly different way of seeing critical constraints and obsolete assumptions.

In the Epilogue, I discuss our family foundation and my family. I may be a genuine workaholic, but family always comes before work. Just ask my wife.

In conclusion, anyone should have the opportunity to read and think about the ideas presented in this autobiography, especially individuals who cannot afford to buy books. This is especially relevant for many students in developing countries who take the Certificate in Value Creation online course offered by the Madden Center. As previously noted, chapters 3, 4, and 5 are already open-access. The preface and overview and chapters 1, 2, and 6 will be posted as open-access working papers on SSRN (Social Science Research Network). The book as a completed package, including a dozen cool photographs, is available on Amazon as hard and soft copy plus Kindle.

CHAPTER 1

Liftoff for a Knowledge-Building and Value-Creation Research Program

Engineering books and boxing gloves

In 1961, I started my freshman year at Cal Poly, located on the central California coast outside of San Luis Obispo. The primary reasons I majored in mechanical engineering were because I was good at math, enjoyed working on cars, and had friends who were engineers and liked their careers. The only physical education class (mandatory at Cal Poly) that fit into my schedule was boxing. Although I had no interest in boxing, I took the class. Our instructor was Tom Lee, coach of Cal Poly's collegiate championship boxing team.

That was the first time I put on boxing gloves. I remember wondering if I had inherited any of my grandfather's athletic genes. My grandfather, Bartley Madden, was a professional boxer for twenty years and in the early 1920s beat the then light heavyweight champion Battling Levinsky in a nontitle match. My grandfather fought mainly heavyweights in order to make more money. He was Irish and invariably gave away weight to bigger heavyweights. He became a fan favorite.

My father told me about an evening when he was with my grandfather at the kitchen table meeting with Jack Kearns, the manager of then heavyweight champ Jack Dempsey, who wanted my grandfather to fight Harry Wills. At that time, Wills, a black fighter, had knocked out most heavyweights and the public wanted to see a Dempsey vs. Wills title fight. Kearns said that Wills would surely beat Dempsey and he will never make that match. Instead, he said Dempsey will fight my grandfather if my grandfather beats Wills. From the microfilm archives, the front-page headline in the *New York Times* for June 9, 1924, was Madden vs. Wills tonight. Wills was forty pounds heavier than my grandfather. The fight lasted the full fifteen rounds and was a real-life version of Rocky. Wills won the decision, but my grandfather won the crowd. The following day, the *New York Times* quoted Jack Kearns asserting that, based on the trouble Wills had with Madden, there was no need for a Dempsey vs. Wills match. For a YouTube video of a segment of the first round, go to 6:40 of "Harry Wills: The Black Panther vs. Firpo, Madden."

Coach Lee asked me to join Cal Poly's boxing team, and as the season progressed, I experienced the satisfaction of becoming good at a demanding sport and the excitement of a boxing crowd. After the season ended, Coach Lee called me into his office and said that he was likely to coach the 1964 Olympic boxing team and that if I committed to train year-round, he could guarantee me a spot in the Olympic trials. I told him without hesitation to count me in. That summer, I met Frankie Goodman, fight manager, trainer, and widely recognized as the preeminent teacher of scientific boxing—I hit you, you miss me. Frankie taught me that every offensive move has a defensive component to it. Frankie became my mentor, and I learned his way of boxing while sparring with professional boxers. Learning his way of boxing became a passion for me. Frankie often said that I was his best student.

At the start of my sophomore year, Cal Poly dropped boxing and I then transferred to the University of Southern California due to their better engineering curriculum. I continued my regular routine of sparring with the pros and learning under Frankie Goodman's critical eye.

I did an internship with the Los Angeles Department of Water and Power (front cover photo was taken when I was an intern) and subsequently was offered a full-time job with a high probability that I would secure a critical skills draft deferment. At that time, the Vietnam war was peaking. Meanwhile, many of Frankie's boxers fought at the Olympic Auditorium in Los Angeles, and the fights were on national television on Friday nights. Two of my boxing peers, Ron Redelsperger and Roland Ryer, scored multiple impressive wins on national TV. As a young man of twenty-two, the thought of winning a fight at the Olympic Auditorium seemed very, very cool.

After receiving my engineering degree in 1965, I worked out in a downtown Los Angeles gym where I became friendly with a retired trainer who had worked with many world-class fighters. One day after sparring with a tough young pro, I started talking with him, thinking he might give me a compliment. Instead, he made an astute observation: "Bart, you do OK with guys who use fifty percent of their athletic ability because you use one hundred and ten percent. You seem smart, so why come around here and take a chance of getting hurt bad?" Even though I easily handled sparring with beginning (four-round preliminary) pro boxers, sparring with highly accomplished professional boxers clearly showed that this was not the best use of my time. That reality check told me to walk away from boxing (and potential serious injury from blows to the head). Go to business school and become an entrepreneur, hopefully gaining the satisfaction of doing well in a different competitive environment. Sounded like a plan. However, I soon received notice that the U.S. Army wanted me to report for active duty.

Basic training at Fort Bliss, Texas, then on to U.C. Berkeley

I started basic training during one especially hot summer in 1966 at Fort Bliss, Texas, and immediately got on the wrong side of my platoon sergeant. I was on one of the point positions for the platoon, and I simply could not understand the marching commands that Sergeant Garcia shouted. He assumed that I must be a wise guy trying to make him look bad. He promised to make life hell for me, and the Sergeant kept his word. Meanwhile, I was encouraged to sign up for Officer Candidate School. After multiple visits with the officer in charge, I respectfully declined and explained my desire for an entrepreneurial life much different than a military life. Fortunately, he and I got along. He indicated that there were a few positions for enlisted men with scientific or engineering degrees and he would look into it for me. If I did not get one of those positions, most likely I would receive orders for infantry Vietnam.

Every day, Sergeant Garcia relentlessly gave me grief. One morning, he announced to the platoon that two of us would participate in one of the scheduled boxing matches later that day. He selected the platoon bully, an-ex high school football player with a Neanderthal-like build and, to no surprise, me. I raised my hand and said I didn't want to box. Garcia said that I had a choice, either put on the gloves or go back to week 1 and take basic training over again. This bully had done something despicable to one of my friends, a little guy who kept to himself. The prior week on an overnight march, the bully urinated in my buddy's canteen and thought that was really funny. Just before the match, my friend was lacing up my gloves, wondering why I was so relaxed and pleading with me to avoid getting hurt. To the noisy crowd, the Neanderthal bully looked formidable, especially next to a skinny opponent who just took off his thick black horn-rimmed glasses. Before the bell, my opponent shouted in my face what he intended to do to me, which seemed amusing to me at that time.

In the middle of the second round, he went down and did not get up for a considerable period of time. The crowd was silent. I did not feel good about what I had done. It was now apparent to me that I had regrettably spent years learning how to efficiently hurt another human being instead of using my time learning how to provide value to customers as described in the business books I had been reading. In addition, my strongest belief was a commitment to do something important with my life. But, given my current circumstances, my life was spiraling downward, especially if my orders said infantry Vietnam.

Meanwhile, life with Sergeant Garcia continued. "Madden, take my cigarette butt and flush it down the toilet." "Yes, sergeant," I replied. "Madden, I don't much like how you just looked at me, gimme fifty (pushups)." "Yes, sergeant," I replied. Days went by slowly. At the end of basic training, everyone in our platoon lined up to receive orders. The person in front of me had a master's degree in mathematics. He got infantry Vietnam as did all the others in front of him. My orders said: scientific and engineering, report to Dugway Proving Grounds in two weeks.

After receiving one of the coveted scientific and engineering positions, I reported to Dugway Proving Grounds, Utah. This is eighty-five miles southwest of Salt Lake City and the site for chemical and biological weapons testing. I had a great civilian boss, Bob Burge, and I worked with other civilian engineers. Bob liked the work I did, and he continued to give me more challenging assignments. One assignment was to fly to Edgewood Arsenal in Aberdeen, Maryland, to explain to a colonel and his staff why Dugway Proving Grounds was not going to grant approval for their tear gas munition. Interesting meeting. Colonels don't much like enlisted soldiers explaining why they can't do what they want to do. From then on, I learned to attend future meetings in a civilian suit, not my Army uniform. I appreciated the challenges Bob put on my desk, including crafting the test plan for the new Army gas mask.

One Friday night at Dugway, my drinking buddies and I were watching the televised boxing matches from the Olympic Auditorium. I mentioned that the tall welterweight has a right hand that could knock down a horse but with a hitch before he throws it, a tell that his opponent could exploit. A loud voice asked, "Madden, how do you know that?" Rather than providing details, I decided to call it a night. Walking back to the barracks, I contemplated my next step, which was graduate business school at the University of California at Berkeley.

After completion of my service, the GI bill and student loans enabled me to attend Berkeley full-time. Two courses there led to a passion for a deeper understanding of how firms create value and the connection to their stock market valuations. I took my first finance course from David Pyle and studied the mathematics of firm valuation and related topics including stock market efficiency (i.e., all relevant valuation information is in the current stock price). My investment course with Victor Niederhoffer focused on market inefficiencies. His way of seeing the world (of stock prices) differed from all my finance textbooks and assigned readings and made a significant impact on me. I became friendly with Victor and followed his career after he left Berkeley. He later became a world champion in professional squash, and his investment gains were legendary, documented in his book, *The Education of a Speculator*. After his book was published, his losses became legendary. These two courses were pure intellectual excitement that dovetailed into a business career researching value creation at the firm level.

Callard Madden & Associates

After I received my MBA in 1969, I accepted a job in the investment research department at Continental Bank in Chicago. An executive at a brokerage firm told my boss, Jim McWilliams, that a security analyst at his firm, Chuck Callard, had ideas for a research program that did not fit his firm's needs. Jim suggested that Chuck and I work together on a trial basis. Six months later, we founded Callard Madden & Associates, and Continental Bank became our first customer. The goal was to advance a commercial research program to go beyond state-of-the-art academic research and deliver insights to enable our money manager clients to make better investment decisions. Chuck Callard was a brilliant economist who had worked in corporate planning and in investment research. He gave me the opportunity to design and write the computer code for what became known as the CFROI (cash-flow-return-on-investment) life-cycle valuation model and related life-cycle track records that were adjusted for inflation, which was on the rise in the early 1970s. Think of the CFROI as a more accurate measure of return-on-capital.

Bob Hendricks was hired to market an admittedly rough initial product for money managers. Bob had all the qualities of both a leader and a marketing genius for understanding client needs; in addition, he was a superb communicator. As Callard Madden expanded, Bob and I worked as a team to build a corporate planning business. With the CFROI valuation model and database, we were able to demonstrate that our approach to the stock market provided new insights to the client regarding stock market valuations for their firm and their competitors. That was the proverbial foot in the door. Typically, projects involved inflation-adjusted performance measurement of the firm and its business units, and strategic analyses as to resource allocations, including analyses of divestitures and acquisition candidates. Bob made the sale and presented the final report to top management and often the board. I did the work in between. We made a great team!

Chuck owned the majority of shares, and while everyone liked him, he was a terrible leader. Way too much of our cash flow invariably was used to fund his expanding portfolio of research projects that were always not quite ready to be commercialized, but according to Chuck, they represented the future of the firm. The rest of us wanted to focus on corporate planning, a subscription service for a global database for money managers, and at an appropriate time, money management. After fourteen years, I left to manage money, followed by the remaining key people who then started HOLT Planning Associates with Bob as managing partner. "HOLT" refers to the first letter of the last names of Bob Hendricks, Eric Olsen, Marvin Lipson, and Rawley Thomas who all left Callard Madden & Associates a year after I had left.

After HOLT's corporate planning business was spun out to the Boston Consulting Group in 1991, the renamed HOLT Value Associates began to prosper. I continued to informally provide research ideas and later rejoined Bob and the team full time. Prior to HOLT being acquired, a startup money management business was spun out as Ironbridge Capital Management. In 2002, HOLT was acquired by Credit Suisse for $100 million. In 2003, I took early retirement to start a new career. Today, the HOLT Global database is used by many large money management organizations worldwide.

The life-cycle framework

During an intense four-month period in 1971 at Callard Madden & Associates, I developed the CFROI metric as part of building from scratch a comprehensive model of a firm that included life-cycle valuation mathematics.[1] Those were the days of Fortran (an engineering programming language that I knew quite well) and punched cards for computer programs. Every morning, I would wake up early and take the Chicago "L" train to the computer center at Northwestern University, north of Chicago. Late at night, I would arrive at Mother's, a famous tavern in Chicago close to my apartment. After a cheeseburger and a beer, I would then lug my box of computer cards to my apartment to sleep before beginning the cycle again. This was pure intellectual fun.

In this section, I describe the life-cycle framework that offers insights to boards of directors, management, and investors. It is simple and intuitive. After you gain some experience with life-cycle track records, my bet is that you will then view any history of a firm as deficient if it does not display the firm's life-cycle track record.

The usefulness of the life-cycle lens to dissect a firm's past history is illustrated in chapter 4 for Deere (diversified farm manufacturer) and in chapter 5 for Cummins (engines and power generation). How can investors interpret the blizzard of information that engulfs individual firms? The life-cycle framework offers a guidepost for interpreting short-term news in the context of what, if any, economic effects impact a firm's market valuation rooted in long-term life-cycle performance.[2]

My adoption of the life-cycle framework began in business school after I read *Capital and Rates of Return in Manufacturing Industries* by the Nobel Laureate economist George Stigler. He emphasized:

> There is no more important proposition in economic theory than that, under competition, the rate of return on investment tends towards equality in all industries. Entrepreneurs will seek to leave relatively unprofitable industries and enter relatively profitable industries.[3]

The figure below, which spotlights Stigler's viewpoint, makes intuitive sense to experienced businesspeople while capturing in two variables the source of future net cash receipts that ultimately drive stock market valuations: (1) a firm's *economic returns* (think return-on-capital), and (2) its *reinvestment rates* change over time due to the interplay of skill and competition plus the fact that the firm is growing larger over time. The firm is part of an economic system.

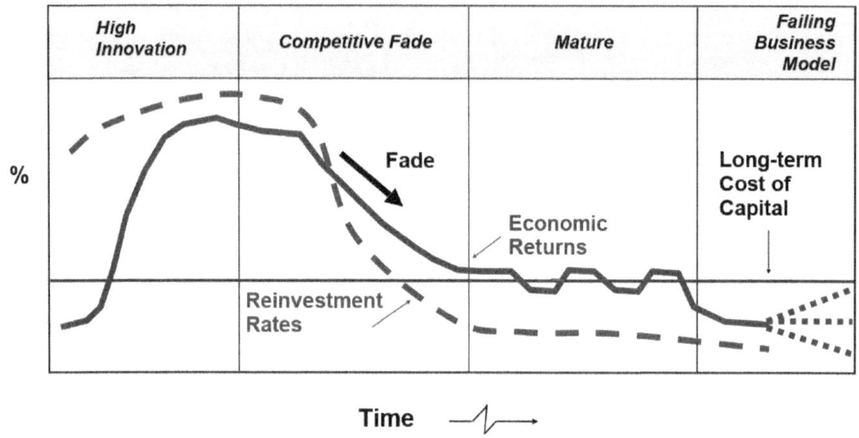

Figure 1.1 The life-cycle framework
Source: Madden (2020), p. 86.

Let's take a moment to review the four stages in the competitive life-cycle framework. In the *high innovation* stage, entrepreneurs who commit their lives to startup firms are often pressured to quickly show a profit. A more important imperative is to quickly either confirm the core assumptions underpinning the business model or to pivot, using knowledge gained, to a revised business model. An innovative business model that earns economic returns well in excess of the cost of capital is an important achievement. Ideally, the business can scale and high economic returns are matched by high reinvestment rates, thereby creating significant appreciation in the firm's market valuation. That combination is a magnet for competitors to attempt to duplicate or improve upon the customer experience delivered by the firm that has now transitioned from a startup to the next life-cycle stage.

In the *competitive fade* stage, investors tend to focus on perceived competitive advantage. Business books discuss competitive advantage as if the firm is an isolated fortress surrounded by a moat—the deeper and wider the better. However, competition is continually at work, which, over time, results in economic returns fading toward the cost of capital and reinvestment rates fading to much slower growth rates (see fade in the above figure). The New Economy has brought forth platform businesses (e.g., Google, Amazon, etc.). Their network effects make the platform more valuable as more customers use it. That is a prescription for exceedingly favorable fade for those firms who control the platform. In general, the key to favorable fade is a knowledge-building proficiency (culture) that is superior to competitors. For example, lean thinking is an application of systems thinking with a well-deserved reputation of rooting out waste (i.e., activities that do not add value).

Nurturing and sustaining a knowledge-building culture entails a commitment by, and continual involvement of, top management. The commitment is to give people the freedom to creatively think and to transfer decision rights (with related responsibilities) to those with the best knowledge for the task at hand. Creative thinking leads to new products and services that often require the firm to build or acquire new capabilities. The old adage "stick to the knitting" is a recipe for fast fade.

Excessive bureaucracy is the hallmark of fade that positions the firm in the *mature* stage of the life cycle. Most large businesses are typically managed with a command-and-control hierarchical structure. They are prime targets for consulting firms who offer advice on digital transformations, AI implementation, etc. However, these initiatives are natural extensions of systems thinking. The consulting firms rarely recommend that top management and boards of directors need to have personnel who are well-versed in systems thinking to better enable adaptation to a fast-changing world. There is a value-creation opportunity for large firms to transition to flatter organizational structures that can eliminate bureaucracy and complacency.

The hallmark of the *failing business model* stage is extensive and deeply entrenched bureaucracy and complacency. Management and the board are not just slow in adapting to the rapid changes in the environment—but much worse: they fail to perceive the need to change. Typically, restructuring is needed that includes new management and new board members.

After decades of studying life-cycle track records, I believe a stake in the ground is warranted. The critical determinant of a firm's long-term performance is its knowledge-building proficiency relative to competitors, which is discussed in the next chapter.

How do I know what I think I know?

I have become one of Amazon's best customers for books related to my three passions: business performance and valuation, systems thinking, and knowledge building. My library is organized around approximately fifty key topics with color codes identifying especially important books. References in the important books lead to a never-ending stream of academic journal articles for daily reading. Periodic purging of less important books makes room for the new ones. I also consume a variety of science and business publications that provide leads on new books. I have mastered the art of fast and efficient skimming in order to pinpoint important stuff that I then carefully read. I probably go through twenty books before I encounter one worth reading cover to cover.

I spent considerable time reading what philosophers have to say about a personally intriguing question: How do I know what I think I know? This proved to be a low return on my invested time with the exception of books by the philosopher John Dewey. His book with Arthur Bentley, *Knowing and the Known*, is insightful but extraordinarily dense and a true challenge to read due to its hyper concern for precision in language and abstraction. My reading of Dewey led me, in turn, to an obscure but fascinating book called *The Morning Notes of Adelbert Ames Jr.* that contains correspondence between Ames and Dewey discussing the powerful visual demonstrations devised by Ames and much more. I then consumed everything in print about Ames. Dewey said about Ames: "I think your work is by far the most important work done in the psychological-philosophical field during this century."[4]

Adelbert Ames Jr.

Ames was the first to provide convincing evidence of the shortcomings of the conventional view of perception—that is, the brain passively taking sensory inputs through the eyes and processing the reality "out there," so that the end result mimics how a camera processes an image. The conventional view continued throughout the twentieth century and was heavily influenced by the neuroscientist David Marr's work on the processing of visual information.[5] Ames argued that language was inadequate for communicating his ideas—hence, the importance of visual demonstrations so that others could experience what he wanted to communicate.

I eagerly embraced the way Ames, through his demonstrations, showed that our assumptions, rooted in past experiences, heavily influence the perceptual experience. I flew to San Francisco to personally experience many of these ingenious demonstrations, which were then displayed at the Exploratorium, a museum for science, art, and human perception.

The most famous demonstration, still described in modern psychology textbooks, is the Ames Room. I looked through a peephole with one eye at a specially constructed room and perceived people inside being radically different in height. Even though I was aware of the room's unusual construction, my brain could not purge the assumptions of level floors, rectangular walls, etc. On the one hand, I could conclude that my perception distorts reality. On the other hand, a more insightful conclusion is that the Ames Room demonstrates the strong pull of our assumptions in shaping the reality we perceive. Observers can't break through their assumptive worlds (a term Ames used frequently) by just abstract thinking. However, if one practices throwing a ball and touching parts of the room with a stick, a new "reality" emerges. We alter deeply imbedded assumptions through feedback.

Discovering Ames was a major stake in the ground for me in better understanding the knowing (perceiving) process. One needs to be continually on guard for the strong and silent pull of assumptions, especially those that we never question, of which there are a lot. But of course, the scientific method overcomes the potential biases as to how a problem is formulated and how data are collected and analyzed. Right? Well, not quite. The opinion of the economist Edward Leamer concerning many journal articles rings true:

> The econometric art as it is practiced at the computer terminal involves fitting many, perhaps thousands of statistical models. One or several that the researcher finds pleasing are selected for reporting purposes. This searching for a model is often well intentioned, but there can be no doubt that such a specification search invalidates the traditional theories of inference. The concepts of unbiasedness, consistency, efficiency, maximum-likelihood estimation, in fact, all the concepts of traditional theory, utterly lose their meaning by the time an applied researcher pulls from the bramble of computer output the one thorn of a model he likes best, the one he chooses to portray as a rose.[6]

Dewey and Ames shared a *transactional* view of scientific inquiry in which reality exists in the context of purposeful human behavior.[7]

This view does not require the denial of a real world; rather, it explicitly recognizes our participation in shaping the world that we see as real.

During the 1980s, I intensely studied Dewey and Ames, along with a wide variety of material on knowledge building. For example, Dewey's approach to knowing has some similarity to Karl Popper in that both reject certainty and promote a process of learning from errors as part of knowledge building.

Ames was an eccentric genius who started as a lawyer, transitioned to a painter, and finally settled on researching vision. Note the word *becomingness* in the biography of Ames by W. C. Bamberger, *Adelbert Ames, Jr.: A Life of Vision and Becomingness*. Ames believed that we are continually remaking ourselves in a state of becomingness. Moreover, our foundational beliefs about a purposeful life are instrumental in orchestrating these continual, often imperceptible changes to who we are. This is a powerful idea. How might it be used?

Let's consider how value creation is defined in the context of business firms. A firm creates value if it can efficiently deliver products and services addressing even mundane but essential needs (water, food). Innovative products and services (mobile phones, the internet) can enable vastly improved experiences versus the old way. In both situations, value is created when customers say about their experiences (including the cost to acquire), "this is a good deal."

Shifting to Ames, with his emphasis on becomingness, spotlights how value creation extends beyond business firms and economic transactions. Individuals can create value for you by either improving your concept of a purposeful life or by affecting your becomingness in a way that advances your journey on a purposeful life. For example, an older person provides sage advice to a younger person as to a career path that is well-suited to the younger person's interests and talents and that most likely will upgrade that person's skill as a value creator.

A transactional approach to economic research

Our participation in shaping the world that we see had a big impact on how I thought about knowledge building. As my thinking progressed, I started working on a paper that summarized what I had learned. Eventually, "A Transactional Approach to Economic Research" (1991) was published in the *Journal of Socio-Economics*.

Here is one example that I crafted in the article addressing the troublesome notion of reality. Consider a *blue mailbox made of steel* that would appear to be an independent thing. In general, giving names to things fosters a belief in an independent reality. However, a transactional approach asserts that the mailbox attribute *blue* can't mean the same to a blind person as it does to a person of normal vision. Similarly, the hardness of steel involves making a comparison. And to further argue against an independent reality, if I put the mailbox in the basement, it no longer would (function as) be a mailbox. To reiterate, we participate in shaping the world that we see as real.

Two sections of this paper led to correspondence with two Nobel Laureate economists, which in turn gave me confidence that the article did present useful ideas. First, in the article I reviewed the importance of experimental economics, a field pioneered by Vernon Smith and for which he was awarded a Nobel Prize. Experimental economics is an innovative process of blending feedback data with theory appraisals. Experimenters can confirm or disconfirm the behavioral assumptions of a theory using laboratory controls for environment and institutions.

I sent the paper to Vernon Smith. He wrote back a detailed letter (March 28, 1988) noting that ". . . your treatment brings an illumination to the idea [past experiences and perceptions] that I had not seen. I found your discussion here particularly valuable." Bingo! I now see how a nonacademic and a non-PhD like me can build up a network of top academics willing to critique my work (as long as I provide material that they find insightful). My often-repeated routine is to send a working paper with an introductory letter to prospective members of my network. The letter needs to communicate that I have studied their work and have referenced one of their articles related to my paper, explain how my paper connects to their work, and ask for comments and criticisms.

Vernon and I became good friends, and I joined his advisory board. I had heard that Vernon loved to fish but for years did not have available time since he works seven days a week, every week. I had recently caught a big bass at our summer home in Valparaiso, Indiana. My wife, Maricela, took a great photo of me holding up the bass next to our daughters, Lucinda and Miranda. I sent the photo to Vernon and suggested that he and I should do some serious fishing at our lake. A few weeks later, Vernon and his wife, Candace, arrived for a three-day visit. That became an annual event for many years. The first time Vernon and I took my boat out, we spent a half-day fishing, and he caught twice as many bass as I did. Same result the next day. I soon found myself copying everything Vernon did from the squiggly artificial purple worm he used to how he retrieved this lure. It worked.

The methodology of positive economics

Shifting to the paper's second section of interest, one of the most famous essays in economics (and certainly one of the most influential) is Milton Friedman's "The Methodology of Positive Economics" (1953). Friedman's main point was that a theory's validity should not be judged by the realism of its underlying assumptions but rather by the accuracy of its predictions. In effect, theories should be viewed "as if" their assumptions were true.

Although this essay generated enormous controversy, Friedman chose never to formally respond to his critics or to further write on methodology. As a result, there has been a never-ending debate as to what

Friedman "really believes" on this topic and whether his approach helps or harms research in economics and related disciplines, such as finance.

It can be argued that with complex economic phenomena, much can be learned by organizing and studying data as if certain assumptions applied. This learning opportunity need not be abandoned, even when certain assumptions are shown to be inaccurate. The difficulty lies in generalizing Friedman's approach as a preferred methodology for improving economic theory. Researchers implementing Friedman's methodology can all too easily construct theory by transforming strongly held beliefs from their assumptive worlds into unrealistic assumptions. They believe that their theory's assumptions should be viewed as descriptions as if true. Prediction is the ultimate proving ground and criticism of assumptions is not relevant, so they say. Constructive skepticism toward particular assumptions is labeled as a misguided attempt to question the realism of assumptions.

I understand the usefulness of higher math in engineering in order to solve problems that otherwise could not be solved. I remember an experiment in my fluid dynamics class in which my observation seemed to violate common sense. Yet, using Bernoulli's principle, I could mathematically derive that the strange result did in fact make sense, once I understood the physical process explained by the math. Practical people (engineers) are quick to pick up mathematical insights *if this helps them solve problems*. Do the majority of the highly mathematical papers in economics and finance bring practical insights that could not otherwise be obtained? I side with the Nobel Laureate economist Ronald Coase:

> Economics has been becoming more and more abstract, less and less related to what goes on in the real world. In fact, economists have devoted themselves to studying imaginary systems, and they don't distinguish between the imaginary system and the real world. That's what modern economics has

> been and continues to be. All the prestige goes to people who produce the most abstract results about an economic system that doesn't exist.[8]

Model builders can point out that since I personally do not build highly mathematical models, I'm by definition sitting in the bleachers and don't understand what the mathematical modelers on the field are doing. I disagree and refer to the views of Professor Paul Pfleiderer at Stanford University. He is a highly regarded builder of mathematical finance models. In his paper "Chameleons: The Misuse of Theoretical Models in Finance and Economics," he wrote:

> A model becomes a chameleon when it is built on assumptions with dubious connections to the real world but nevertheless has conclusions that are uncritically (or not critically enough) applied to understanding our economy. . . . chameleons are created and nurtured by the mistaken notion that one should not judge a model by its assumptions . . . and by misplaced appeals to "as if" arguments, elegance, subtlety, assumptions that are "standard in the literature". . .[9]

In the final section of my paper, my key argument against the methodology of positive economics was distilled into this example. Consider the following theory's superb record for prediction about when water will freeze or boil. The theory says that water behaves *as if* there were a water devil who gets angry at 32 degrees and 212 degrees Fahrenheit and alters the chemical state accordingly to ice or steam. In a superficial sense, the water-devil theory is successful for the immediate problem at hand. But the molecular insight that water is comprised of two molecules of hydrogen and one molecule of oxygen not only led to predictive success but also led to the growth of modern chemistry.

In a letter dated April 3, 1990, Friedman noted: ". . . your final section, I have no quarrel with it, and it has no quarrel with me, so let us leave it at that." My interpretation is that in his own research, Friedman took care in avoiding speculative mathematical extrapolations from a base of unrealistic assumptions. However, such is not the case with many other researchers who have a passion for high-level math and use Friedman's methodology as a rationale to continue doing what they enjoy doing.

Worldviews and business performance

As my thinking about knowledge building evolved, I increasingly focused on the importance of one's worldview and the role of language in obfuscating assumptions. In 2012, my article "Management's Worldview: Four Critical Points About Reality, Language, and Knowledge Building to Improve Organization Performance" was published. My purpose was to illustrate how my work was relevant to business firm performance (i.e., why knowledge building can uncover insights about firm performance and especially innovation).

I told two stories in my 2012 article that illustrated how I was seeing the world with an eye on the knowledge-building process. I was asking deeper questions about strategy, innovation, culture, etc. as part of analyzing a firm's long-term track record.

The first story dissects Walmart outperforming the S&P 500 one hundredfold during the period 1970 to 1990. How and why did this happen? In my *Value Creation Thinking* book, I investigated Walmart's investor expectations and subsequent life-cycle performance.[10] The major surprise was the sustained, extraordinarily high reinvestment rates coupled to economic returns well above the cost of capital. How did this happen?

The answer is contained in a single word—store. In the early 1970s,

Kmart was the number-one U.S. retailer. In their annual reports, management extolled their business model that gave exceptional autonomy and responsibility to store managers who were obviously close to customers. Kmart management's worldview was rooted in the belief that future success depended upon their execution of this proven business model. However, the CEO of a small retailer in Arkansas, Sam Walton, concluded that a store was a node in a network.[11] That changes everything. Distribution centers could be strategically located so that Walmart stores could efficiently serve communities outside of big cities, with centralized ordering based on monitoring store inventories, etc. In the early 1980s, I was researching Walmart and wrote Walton a letter inquiring if he really utilized systems thinking from the beginning. A week later, I received a reply: "Dear Bart, Yes!!!" Walmart eventually drove Kmart into bankruptcy. Our competitive free-market economic system enables entrepreneurs to radically reshape industries while creating value for all the firm's stakeholders. A sharply different conceptualization of store originated with Jeff Bezos, who, as everyone knows, went on to create Amazon.

My second story describes the knowledge building of Dr. Edward Jenner (1749-1823) during the twenty years he spent learning about smallpox. In his day, if you didn't die after contracting smallpox, you were terribly scarred and often blind. His work led to the first preventative vaccination and, finally, the eradication of smallpox. Jenner's mentor was John Hunter, a top scientist who instilled in Jenner the need to develop hypotheses that challenge the status quo and to relentlessly experiment.

The medical establishment and Jenner had different worldviews that were spotlighted by their different reactions to reports from milkmaids claiming that they didn't get smallpox because they had a prior exposure to cowpox. The establishment discarded this idea because not all milkmaids who contracted cowpox were able to avoid smallpox. At a deeper level, the establishment could not conceive of the possibility that a cow disease could protect against a human disease.

Jenner focused initially on language, specifically, the word *exposure.* From milking cows, milkmaids occasionally got pus-filled blisters on their hands lasting a few weeks. This was called cowpox. With Jenner's scientific skepticism, he was aware that our perception of reality and language are intertwined. Therefore, he investigated the meaning of exposure and through extensive experiments learned that there were many cowpox-like diseases, but only one involved the pus that could protect against smallpox. In addition, he learned that the large, bluish blisters that occurred midway through the cowpox cycle had pus potent enough to protect against smallpox. Before Edward Jenner died in 1823, the medical establishment had enthusiastically accepted his findings due to their demonstrated effectiveness. In 1967, the World Health Organization began a campaign to totally eradicate smallpox, which was achieved in 1977.

In 2012, I wrote a monograph, *Reconstructing Your Worldview: The Four Core Beliefs You Need to Solve Complex Business Problems*, to summarize what I had learned. By this time, I had perfected my introductory letter to an art. Top academics have a high level of curiosity that I utilized in my letters to entice them to take a look at what I sent and hopefully provide feedback. I mailed the first draft of the monograph to Edmund Phelps, a highly creative economist who was awarded the Nobel Prize. I asked Phelps for comments and—this is a heavy lift—an endorsement for the not-yet-published monograph. He subsequently used the monograph in a seminar for economics PhD students at Columbia University. I then received this endorsement: "This fine book is a down-to-earth primer on what every businessperson in a dynamic economy needs to know about modern knowledge in economics, psychology, and philosophy." I felt good about that endorsement because it was earned and it demonstrated that I had surmounted the handicap of not being a member of the academic community.

Edmund Phelps became a friend, and I joined his advisory board for the Center on Capitalism and Society at Columbia University. I also benefitted from reading his books describing dynamism—a critical ingredient for economic progress and detailed in the first chapter of my *Value Creation Principles.*

In concluding my monograph, I challenged readers to find situations ripe for innovative thinking. In particular, look for:

- blind acceptance of the system goal as currently specified
- strongly held assumptions that were formulated in an environment far different from today and have become etched in stone
- excessive focus on local optimization.

NOTES

Notes 1 and 2 are more meaningful for readers who are well versed in financial (accounting) performance measurement and discounted cash flow valuation models.

[1] Keep in mind that the firm can be viewed as a portfolio of ongoing projects or investments. At a point in time, the economic return is the average internal rate of return (IRR) of those ongoing investments based on cash outflows and cash inflows. We can't directly measure economic returns. Consequently, we use proxies, ROIC (return-on-invested-capital) and, with minor details changed, RONA (return-on-net-assets). ROIC and RONA have well-known (and less well-known) measurement problems based on the use of net assets. These return metrics are not adjusted for inflation. I developed the CFROI metric to circumvent these measurement problems and also to adjust for inflation. For those interested in these issues, the full story is in a forthcoming SSRN working paper I am writing with Donn DeMuro, "Bridging the Gap Between Accounting Returns and Economic Returns with New Software." The new software provides a practical tool for experimenting with the capitalization and amortization of intangibles outlays and a life-cycle forecasting process to explicitly quantify the value of a firm's future investments.

The life-cycle valuation model is discounted cash flow applied to a future net cash receipt stream generated by a forecast of economic returns and reinvestment rates. All variables are inflation adjusted, meaning that they are in constant dollars (real). A major benefit occurs from the use of life-cycle track records constructed with real CFROIs and real reinvestment rates when the historical period experienced inflation. Since CFROIs are inflation adjusted, their levels and trends improve assessments of economic returns. This, in turn, leads to more informed forecasts as inputs to the life-cycle valuation model.

[2] How does one assign a discount rate in calculating a net present value of a forecasted future net cash receipt stream? Modern finance textbooks ostensibly offer the Capital Asset Pricing Model approach for estimating a firm's cost of capital (discount rate), but this is of zero practical value. In the mid-1970s, the research program at Callard Madden & Associates developed a realistic alternative. Chuck Callard originated the market-implied discount rate approximately three decades before it appeared in academic journals (see chapter 4 and appendix A in my *CFROI Valuation: A Total System Approach to Valuing the Firm*.) In a nutshell, apply the life-cycle valuation model to a large universe of firms where a firm's calculated value is warranted by the forecasted future life cycle of economic returns and reinvestment rates. We want warranted values to be close to actual stock prices. Based on extensive empirical testing of financial characteristics of firms and their actual fade rates, our forecast future fade rates were in good shape. See my "The CFROI Life Cycle" in the *Journal of Investing* (1996) for early empirical fade work that was later supported by extensive econometric research by HOLT Value Associates.

The question then becomes, at a point in time, what investor discount rates should be assigned to individual firms? With a large universe of firms, we can calculate market-implied discount rates. That is, for known market values for firms and known forecast net cash receipts via fade rates for economic returns and reinvestment rates, discount rates are calculated that match the known market values for firms. In my "The CFROI Valuation Model," *Journal of Investing* (1998), a large universe of firms showed particularly strong statistical relationships for *two risk variables* with market-implied discount rates: higher discount rates for smaller firms and higher discount rates for firms with substantial financial leverage (expected since CFROIs include the benefit of interest payments being tax deductible). Hence, firm-specific discount rates could then be calculated at any point in time and are consistent with the forecast procedures (fade rates) that generate the net cash receipts. Such systems thinking has been ignored by conventional textbooks that parachute a discount rate into a valuation model and mush ahead, so to speak.

[3] George Stigler. 1963. *Capital and Rates of Return in Manufacturing Industries*. Princeton, NJ: Princeton University Press. p. 34.

[4] Hadley Cantril. Ed. 1960. *The Morning Notes of Adelbert Ames Jr.*" p. *v*.

[5] Lucia M. Vaina and Richard E. Passingham. Ed. 2017. *Computational Theories and Their Implementation in the Brain: The Legacy of David Marr*. Oxford: Oxford University Press.

[6] Edward E. Leamer. 1983. "Let's Take the Con Out of Econometrics." *American Economic Review*. 73(1): 31-43.

[7] Social scientists focus on the *causes* of human behavior, but a much different approach has been grabbing attention—Perceptual Control Theory (PCT). The key concept is that your brain controls input perceptions through actions to reduce the discrepancy between what you are experiencing and what you want to experience. Behavior is *control of perception*. PCT leads to insights that can help management achieve a firm's purpose through improvements in productivity, employee job satisfaction, and win-win relationships. In 2021, I wrote a monograph, *A Foundational Explanation of Human Behavior: How to Get Beyond Observed Behavior to the Why of What We Do*, that describes the development of PCT. See also Richard S. Marken (2021) *The Study of Living Control Systems: A Guide to Doing Research on Purpose*.

[8] Thomas W. Hazlett. 1999. "Looking for Results: An Interview with Ronald Coase." *Reason*.

[9] Paul Pfleiderer. 2020. "Chameleons: The Misuse of Theoretical Models in Finance and Economics." *Economics* 87, p. 81.

[10] Bartley J. Madden. 2016. *Value Creation Thinking*. Naperville, IL: LearningWhatWorks. pp. 131–133.

[11] Richard P. Rumelt. 2011. *Good Strategy Bad Strategy: The Difference and Why It Matters*. New York: Crown Business. pp. 23-28.

My grandfather, Bartley Madden, 1925. He defeated many leading heavyweights of his era.

Cal Poly boxing team, 1961. Coach Tom Lee is second row, far left. I am first row, far right.

Forbes

September 9, 1996

Bob Hendricks and Bart Madden of HOLT

MONEY & INVESTMENTS

THE MONEY MEN

Follow the cash

HOLT Associates hated Wal-Mart in 1991.
Its unique valuation system tells HOLT to love Wal-Mart now.

From a *Forbes* September 9, 1996, article about HOLT Value Associates. I am on the right. Bob Hendricks is on the left.

Fishing was good at our place in Valparaiso, Indiana. Lucinda, me, and Miranda, 2006.

Candace and Vernon Smith, Maricela, and me, 2006.

CHAPTER 2

The Knowledge Building Loop and Critical Managerial Tasks: Life Lessons for Every Business

The Knowledge Building Loop

This chapter focuses on my journey to better understand knowledge building. I'll argue that knowledge-building proficiency is the foundation for management to deliver sustained value creation. I will offer a holistic framework for knowledge building and value creation that all can use.

To be a value creator means being actively engaged with knowledge building. Here is Edward Hess hitting the nail on the head:

> By detaching our self-image and self-worth from our beliefs, we should be more willing to stress test those beliefs instead of habitually defending them. This means that being who we are won't be tied up in maintaining a particular view, answer, opinion, or conclusion. Rather, we can define our "being" by

how we think and converse. Defining everything we know as conditional—subject to change based on new evidence—can decouple our egos from our beliefs.[1]

Before getting into chapter details, keep in mind these four guideposts:

- Our brains have evolved to rely on past experiences to shape perceptions of what is "out there." We see what our brains tell us to see.
- In order to effectively navigate our daily lives, we experience the world as an objective, independent reality. Language reinforces both our perception of an independent reality and linear cause and effect (noun-verb-noun). Our word choice can subtly separate subject vs. object, organism vs. environment, and observer vs. observed.
- In dealing with complex problems, we must improve our language in order to more accurately analyze interrelationships that are woven into the fabric of complex systems.
- The connection between knowledge building and value creation extends from the individual to the firm and then all the way up to society's economic prosperity.

Eric Beinhocker and Nick Hanauer highlight the fundamental cause of prosperity as I see it:

> . . . markets are evolutionary systems that each day carry out millions of simultaneous experiments [traversing the Knowledge Building Loop] on ways to make our lives better. In other words, *the essential role of capitalism is not allocation—it is* [value] *creation.* Life isn't drastically better for billions of people today than it was in 1800 because we are allocating

> the resources of the 19th-century economy more efficiently. Rather, it is better because we have life-saving antibiotics, indoor plumbing, motorized transport, access to vast amounts of information, and an enormous number of technical and social innovations that have become available to much (if not yet all) of the world's population. The genius of capitalism is that it both creates incentives for solving human problems and makes those solutions widely available [knowledge base]. And it is solutions to human problems that define prosperity, not money.[2] (italics in the original)

Over the years, I have developed a way of connecting components of the knowing process that I label the Knowledge Building Loop (Figure 2.1). It is particularly useful in formulating economic/business problems and in developing solutions consistent with systems thinking. Importantly, it facilitates insightful answers to better questions. There is no predetermined starting point in Figure 2.1 because we continuously traverse the loop in order to both develop and achieve our purposes.

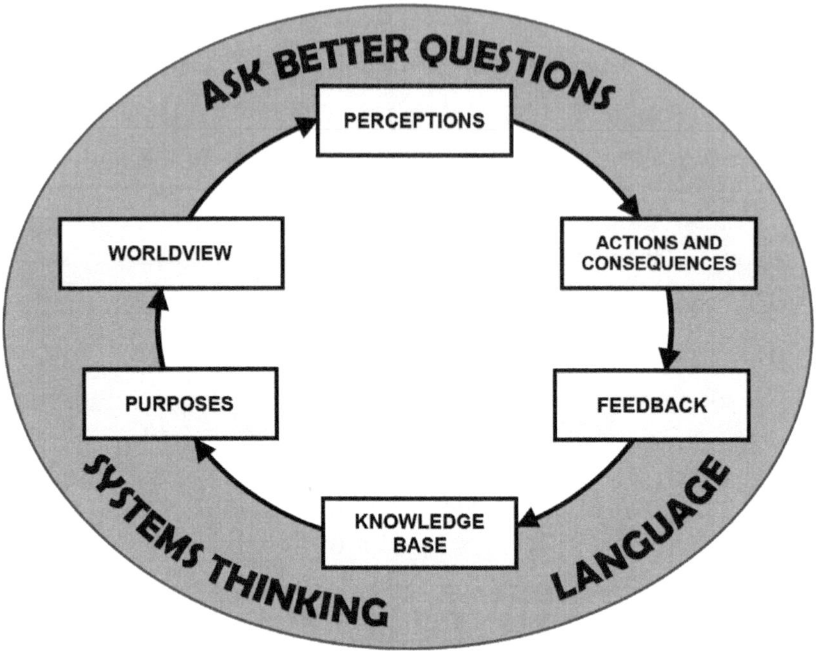

Figure 2.1 The Knowledge Building Loop
Source: The original version of this figure appeared in my 2012 article "Management's Worldview: Four Critical Points about Reality, Language, and Knowledge Building to Improve Organizational Performance."[3]

Our *knowledge base* consists of one's assumptions, which convey intrinsic and ubiquitous uncertainty better than "beliefs" or "truths." These assumptions have varying degrees of reliability that are revealed as one continually traverses the Knowledge Building Loop.

Purposes inform us about what we need to control in order to survive; to specifically take care of ourselves, family, and friends; and to hopefully gain satisfaction from a life worth living. These higher order variables orchestrate control of lower-level variables, such as performing well at work.

One's *worldview* contains the ideas and strongly held beliefs that guide how we interpret and interact with the world. Let's, for example, consider two commonly held worldviews in business. First, lean thinking sees businesses as value streams that contain waste—any activity (including unused time) that does not add value for the customer—that needs to be purged. Second, the theory of constraints sees businesses as systems that have key constraints that are the leverage points to improve overall system performance.

The theory of constraints was developed by Eli Goldratt, who authored many business novels, such as *The Goal*, a mega bestseller. In my opinion, his most significant work was in developing logical thinking maps for revealing obsolete assumptions. After I contacted him and explained how our work interconnected, we began an email dialogue. For about a year, we exchanged emails discussing his logical thinking maps and the Knowledge Building Loop. In watching his videos, I noticed that he almost always had a cigar or pipe in hand. We finally met at one of his conferences. During a break, we took a walk, and he laughed that he needed a nicotine fix every three hours. He invited me to Israel for a visit, and it seemed like just a matter of weeks later he was diagnosed with lung cancer and died soon thereafter.

Returning to our discussion of the loop, consider *perceptions*. Our brains have evolved to enable us to act without elaborate analyses of multiple actions and likely consequences. Our brains continually make predictions via analogy to past experiences in order to take actions likely to yield desired consequences.

The *actions* we take and the subsequent *consequences* provide *feedback* by which we accept or reject assumptions. When working on a problem, actions based on a hunch about the root cause of a problem can yield consequences that provide feedback that changes our knowledge base.

As to how our brains perceive, there is a famous experiment available on YouTube, "Selective Attention Test," that involves people observing individuals passing a basketball and the observers are instructed to count the number of passes. A person dressed in a gorilla suit walks by, yet most individuals do not perceive the gorilla. The conventional conclusion is that not only are people blind to the obvious but they also do not comprehend that they are blind. However logical this may seem, it is not accurate. Teppo Felin offers a more insightful and compelling analysis:

> . . . what people are looking *for*—rather than what people are merely looking *at*—determines what is obvious. . . . Knowing what to observe, what might be relevant and what data to gather in the first place is not a computational task—it's a human one. . . . Humans do a remarkable job of generating questions, expectations, hypotheses and theories that direct awareness and attention toward what is relevant, useful and novel. And it is these—generative and creative—qualities of the human mind that deserve further attention. After all, these and related aspects of the mind are surely responsible for the significant creativity, technological advances, innovation and large-scale flourishing that we readily observe around us.[4] (italics in the original)

I agree with Felin's inside-out view of perception, which is consistent with the interrelationships of purposes, worldview, and perceptions in the Knowledge Building Loop. In addition, it emphasizes the core finding of Adelbert Ames, discussed in chapter 1, about the role of past experiences in shaping perception.

Statistical testing and academic research

Individuals can recognize faulty assumptions quicker than organizations, according to Bill Starbuck, the former editor of the highly rated *Administrative Science Quarterly*, coeditor of the Oxford University Press *Handbook of Organizational Design* (two volumes), and a recipient of the 2005 Academy of Management Distinguished Scholarly

Contributions Award. Starbuck stresses the long memory of organizations with assumptions baked into the firm's operating procedures and culture—assumptions that have proven reliable in driving past successes. Technologies change, social trends gain momentum, and in a changed environment, key assumptions of one's business model can easily become obsolete. To effectively handle the situation, unlearning is required. Organizations tend to do that slowly.

Starbuck is arguably the most insightful and scathing critic of research in the social sciences in general and business management in particular. His *The Production of Knowledge: The Challenge of Social Science Research* emphasizes that researchers do what advances their careers rather than creating new useful knowledge. The workhorse for empirical journal articles, which is the path to gaining tenure and career advancement, is multiple regression analysis. Even though these articles typically contain a model that may appear logically sound, Starbuck asserts that in general these articles do not contribute to new, useful knowledge. The articles lack genuine insights into a causal model of the phenomena under investigation. In reading the following quote, keep in mind that the null hypothesis of a multiple regression is that there is no relationship between the dependent variable and the independent variable(s). Starbuck makes an important point:

> Someone who gathers a large enough sample can be very nearly certain of rejecting a point null hypothesis. . . . social scientists [have misused] statistical significance tests when they acted as if statistical significance indicates the importance of studied phenomena. The importance of phenomena should not depend on how much work a researcher is willing to do.
>
> Statistical education focused on formulations that statisticians developed early in the twentieth century. In the absence of electronic computers, statisticians needed

> to concentrate on functions that they could manipulate algebraically, and they needed an approach to analysis that would allow many different researchers to use the same, generic numerical tables. Point null hypotheses made algebra much simpler, and hypotheses about "no difference" appeared to have applicability to many research situations. One very unfortunate consequence was widespread use of "tests" that were very easy to pass.[5]

For complex systems, Starbuck recommends simple models and simple actions accompanied by predicted consequences so that feedback consists of learning that incrementally improves our knowledge base. This ties back to the *actions and consequences* component of the Knowledge Building Loop and the *feedback* component.

In addition, I agree with Starbuck's endorsement of John Platt's landmark *Science* article, "Strong Inference." Platt argues that significantly greater progress in certain scientific fields (e.g., molecular biology) results from implementation of crucial experiments that demonstrate certain assumptions (theories) are false. In contrast, we observe in the social sciences an inexorable increase in alternative theories, often supported by multiple regression studies with a model whose logic is favored by the authors. However, significant progress in science is built upon constructive skepticism implemented via experiments (empirical tests) capable of excluding one or more hypotheses. The predictions in these experiments are not ones favored by the experimenters (as is customary in the social sciences) but directly connect to the hypotheses.

Systems thinking, language, and asking better questions

These three topics (highlighted in Figure 2.1) are intricately interrelated, which became apparent the more I worked on each topic. Let's begin with the limitations of linear thinking, which is the brain's workhorse because linear thinking conserves energy by blending perception and prediction in a way that orchestrates actions and likely (linear) consequences. However, as problems and opportunities gain in importance, invariably we face complex systems with interdependencies unsuited for linear cause-and-effect analysis. Mike Jackson, a top leader in systems thinking and part of my network for discussing ideas and reviewing papers, calls attention to "wicked" problems:

> What help can decision-makers expect when tackling the "messes" and "wicked problems" that proliferate in this age of complexity? They are usually brought up on classical management theory that emphasizes the need to forecast, plan, organize, lead, and control. This approach relies on there being a predictable future environment in which it is possible to set goals that remain relevant into the foreseeable future; on enough stability to ensure that tasks arranged in a fixed hierarchy continue to deliver efficiency and effectiveness; on a passive and unified workforce; and on a capacity to take control action on the basis of clear measures of success. These assumptions do not hold in the modern world, and classical management theory provides the wrong prescriptions . . . managers are left to preserve with their favorite panacea . . . systems thinking [is] the only appropriate response to complexity.[6]

Systems thinking respects the interconnectedness of the parts while focusing on the relationships between them and emergent properties.

Systems operate within systems with feedback loops that are either self-reinforcing or self-correcting. Systems thinking emphasizes holism and holism emphasizes systems thinking. It urges us to creatively reframe problems in ways that are not possible with reductionism that seeks simple, objective causal relationships.

Creatively reframing problems and devising value creation solutions depends on understanding multiple approaches (viewpoints) for analyzing complex systems and on choosing the approach (or approaches) best suited to the challenges. It would help to have an understanding of the systems approaches that are the most philosophically sound and thoroughly researched plus a solid track record of successful applications. Mike Jackson answers the call with *Critical Systems Thinking and the Management of Complexity*.

The Vanguard Method is one of the ten approaches analyzed by Mike. It focuses on a customer perspective coupled to Vanguard's adaptation to service organizations of lean principles for reducing waste. As a systems approach, it is focused in the extreme with details of how work is organized and improved. The Vanguard Method is an insightful application of systems thinking with impressive results.

The intellectual leader of the Vanguard Method is John Seddon, who began his career as an occupational psychologist. Seddon's firm is legendary for using systems thinking to transition service organizations in order to make large scale improvements in reducing waste and improving customer service. In studying Seddon's way of thinking, I was impressed with his use of language in gaining clarity about what is needed to efficiently satisfy customers. For example, a customer call center has a *value demand* that ties to a customer's problem in need of fixing and a *failure demand* that results from not fixing the problem the first time. Vanguard consultants do not use *roll out*, because it implies that management is imposing their solution to change the work done by others. Rather, they use *roll in*, which involves helping those who do the work to understand faults and devise changes that enable them to control and improve the work that they do.[7]

In a nutshell, Vanguard consultants focus on:

- specifying purpose in customer terms
- organizing work as horizontal flow targeted on producing to satisfy demand (pull not push)
- orchestrating experiences (not lectures or reports) for management to accurately *perceive* the dysfunctions caused by command-and-control geared to controlling accounting costs
- communicating that to improve flow, you need measures of flow in the hands of people who do the work
- improving the organization's capability to handle variety, thereby lowering costs and improving service
- focusing management on the interactions of the components of the system and not the components analyzed in isolation.

Vanguard is fundamentally about helping service organizations improve their skill at fast and effective traversing of the Knowledge Building Loop, which enables learning by those who do the work. The purpose is to satisfy customers. The worldview is rooted in systems thinking and the dysfunctions resulting from command-and-control hierarchies. Perceptions are improved by direct experiences of problems caused by faulty assumptions. Those doing the work are given access to relevant measures of flow so that they can learn what actions lead to desired consequences. Feedback focuses on customer satisfaction, and the knowledge base continually improves because employees have the freedom to improve the process of which they are a part.

Seddon echoes the above points:

The principles for the development of knowledge are:

> integrating measures with work, focusing on purpose, designing work in flow rather than functions, and assuming knowledge is associated with work. If these principles were employed, how would we expect a "knowledge worker" to behave? He or she would be clear about the purpose of work, would have measures related to purpose, would be knowledgeable about the end-to-end work flow and would as a result be in a position to understand and improve the work.[8]

In his book *Freedom from Command & Control*, Seddon asks an important question: What is the job of management? He has a simple yet powerful answer: make work "work" better. Important questions rivet our attention and open the door to a range of good things from better dialogue to breakthrough thinking. However, our educational system strongly favors providing right answers rather than asking the right questions. Truly powerful questions generate hope for the future and imagination in crafting answers, and they are generative by providing a path to additional powerful questions that spur knowledge building that is both useful and exciting.

Let's consider an important insight developed by Rodger L. Martin, former dean of the Rotman School of Management, prolific author, and an experienced strategy consultant. His eureka moment was discovering what he believed to be the most important question in strategy. It began with a consulting assignment to facilitate a dialogue among a diverse group of managers of a mining company. Initially, conversations descended into adversarial position-taking. Martin's eureka moment was: "Rather than have them talk about what they thought was true, ask them to specify what would have to be true for the option on the table to be a fantastic choice."[9] Answering this led to collaboration and real progress because it facilitated putting everyone's strongly held assumptions on hold and being more open to new knowledge that may obsolete one or more of their assumptions. This results in more effectively traversing the Knowledge Building Loop in order to gain new useful knowledge.

Language camouflages assumptions while greatly simplifying the world. The entrepreneurs who started Airbnb asked a simple but powerfully illuminating question: What is a hotel room? This led to a business model in which private residences serve the function of a hotel room. Consider all the classroom learning you have experienced that focused on the right answers while ignoring opportunities afforded by asking better questions.

Here is a better question rarely asked: Is inventory an asset? Accountants say yes. However, managers committed to lean principles perceive inventory as a barometer indicating inefficiencies and waste in the production system. Do you believe that accounting costs can serve as reliable checkpoints for seeking gains in efficiency? From a systems perspective (and often explained by Goldratt), increasing the flow of material into a bottleneck (key constraint) can improve the accounting efficiency at the upstream workstation but worsen the bottleneck downstream and degrade overall system performance. Accounting costs have a hidden assumption of system components being independent of one another. Thinking about the assumptions behind the words is an integral part of asking better questions. Language matters.

Asking better questions is similar to formulating better problem statements to facilitate research that delivers solutions. This is not easy because our brains automatically suggest answers to questions related to our past experience. Useful problem statements are questions that often include specification of the gap between the current state and the desired future state.

More insightful questions and problem formulations are fundamentally about reframing that overcomes strongly held assumptions that block productive inquiry. Isn't this a much-needed skill for CEOs? Hal Gregersen makes an important observation that is especially relevant to CEOs' ability to nurture and sustain a knowledge-building culture:

> When people spend a lot of time in hierarchical organizations, they are rarely encouraged to ask questions of any kind. . . . the keys to surviving and thriving are smart answers. People get ahead by standing and delivering solutions to problems just as they are presented to them. Time goes by, the solutions incrementally improve, and no one has paused to revisit the questions. And who ends up in charge of the operation? Someone who is the product of that process. . . . When I learn of leaders who are the exceptions, they are entrepreneurial founders as opposed to classic risers through the ranks.[10]

A holistic knowledge-building and value-creation system

The ideas presented in this section address the use of the Knowledge Building Loop to improve value-creation skills and, in so doing, offer a path to reorganize learning in business schools. The beginning point is that all significant activities of the firm can be positioned as one of six managerial tasks that involve improving: the firm's knowledge-building culture; strategic thinking; organizational structure; efficiency of existing businesses; innovations for existing and future businesses; and context-specific performance measurement. However, these tasks are deeply interrelated because they share a foundational link to the Knowledge Building Loop as the means for improvement.

Take some time to play with the idea that your knowledge base can be productively changed through repetitive and concerted efforts to apply the Knowledge Building Loop in practical ways, such as seen in John Seddon's Vanguard Method.

Figure 2.2 is a visual summary with arrows in both directions emphasizing the interconnections among critical managerial tasks. The Thinking and Doing System positions the Knowledge Building Loop as the foundation for improving results from doing the specified six managerial tasks.

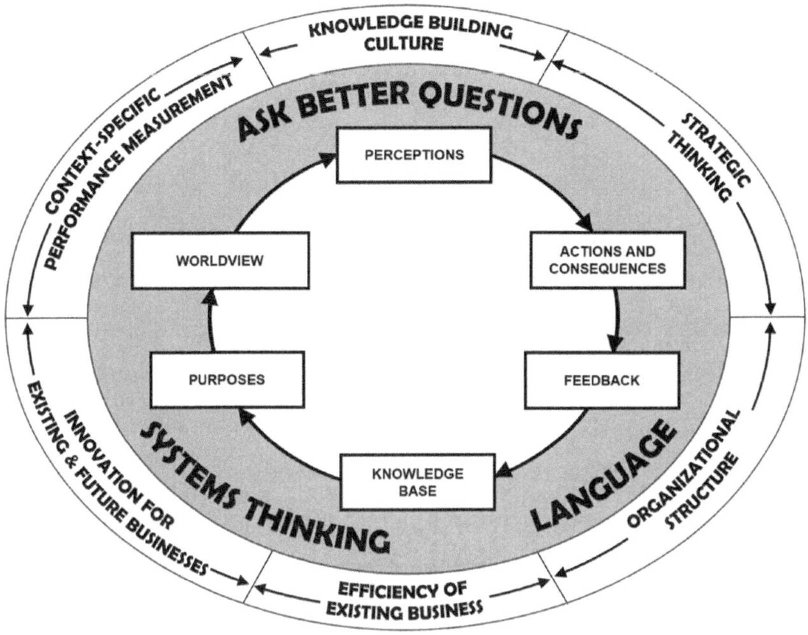

Figure 2.2 Thinking and Doing System

TASK #1: KNOWLEDGE-BUILDING CULTURE

A desirable culture for a firm (or any organization) is rooted in knowledge building with an appreciation for systems thinking, keeping a sharp eye for assumptions behind the words, and asking better questions. Edgar Schein has researched and written extensively about culture in organizations. His book *DEC Is Dead, Long Live DEC: The Lasting Legacy of Digital Equipment Corporation* illustrates how a culture can become frozen due to past successes while management then fails to adapt to a changed environment. The result is rapid passing through the four life-cycle stages described in chapter 1, all the while doing what used to work in the good old days. Schein has a long history of providing insights about a firm's culture:

> . . . a pattern of shared basic assumptions learned by a group as it solved its problems of external adaptation and internal integration, which has worked well enough to be considered valid and, therefore, to be taught to new members as the correct way to perceive, think, and feel in relation to these problems.[11]

Parts of Schein's analysis of the critical components needed for a learning (knowledge building) culture resonate with Mike Jackson's call for diverse approaches for systems thinking to better navigate a fast-changing, complex environment:

> *What must be avoided in the learning culture is the automatic assumption that wisdom and truth reside in any one source or method.* . . . The more diverse cultural resources will be better able to cope with unpredicted events. . . . As the world becomes more complex and interdependent, the ability to think systemically, to analyze fields of forces and understand their joint causal effects on each other, and to abandon simple linear causal logic in favor of complex mental models will become more critical to learning.[12] (italics added)

Try this thought experiment. In one word, what is an important personality characteristic of a CEO that significantly contributes to nurturing and sustaining a knowledge-building culture? If you said humility, you get a gold star. Empirical support for that answer is provided by Amy Ou and her colleagues.[13] They explain that humble CEOs (compared to typical arrogant superstar CEOs) are better at building collaborative teams, sharing information, and involving others in decision-making, orchestrating a widely shared vision, plus their compensation does not reach the head-scratching levels of superstar CEOs. They empirically show that humble-CEO firms outperform superstar-CEO firms. Humble CEOs are much better at gaining cooperation to position the firm to seize opportunities in a changing environment and to simultaneously improve efficiency in existing operations. In a nutshell, get the culture right and it is easier to implement a strategy that adapts to a changing environment. Culture and strategy are interrelated, as emphasized by the two-way arrows in the Thinking and Doing System of Figure 2.2.

TASK #2: STRATEGIC THINKING

Richard Rumelt has a well-earned reputation as a genuine thought leader for strategy due to combining top-notch academic research with decades of consulting. His work has generated a boatload of insights summarized in *The Crux: How Leaders Become Strategists.* He carefully defines the words *goals*, *plans*, and *strategy*. Goals connect to a firm's vision or long-term purpose (i.e., they answer the question: Why are we in business?). Goals are aspirations, not strategy. Plans are the means to coordinate the use of resources. In addition, according to Rumelt, strategy is managing our lack of definitive connections between what we do in the future and what we get in the future. Moreover, strategy leads to actionable steps. Most important, he advises that the group tasked with developing strategy should focus on identifying and understanding challenges and not focus on goals. In particular, focus on those challenges that the firm is capable of handling and that have big value creation upside. That capability can include building or acquiring new skills. Jeff Bezos, the founder of Amazon, makes an important point:

> A much more stable strategy is to start with "What do my customers need?" Then do an inventory of the gaps in your skills. Kindle is a great example. If we set our strategy by what

> our skills happen to be rather than by what our customers need, we never would have done it. We had to go out and hire people who know how to build hardware devices and create a whole new competency for the company.[14]

What about those unpredictables that were not anticipated when the strategy was formulated? They can be managed by a strategy that includes options that are nurtured and ready for action if and when the future favors such options. Moreover, a knowledge-building culture exploits change via fast-paced learning and early adaptation.

Returning to the Knowledge Building Loop and the often-unrecognized impact of purposes, Rumelt highlights one aspect of his consulting experiences:

> It is not group process per se that causes too early convergence on action. It is the habits of viewing strategy as setting overall goals or as decision making among predetermined alternative actions. . . . Most of the time the senior executive had a fixed opinion about the desired outcome, and that outcome was closely attached to only one or two conceivable actions. . . . These predetermined *purposes*, not a defect in the group process, made collective reflection impossible.[15] (italics added)

Capitalizing on Rumelt's insights, a useful definition of strategic thinking is: Traversing the Knowledge Building Loop with constructive skepticism about key assumptions, an eye for systems (ecosystems), and asking better questions; identifying challenges that we can handle by focusing on what we will do and not do; and organizing feedback attuned to changes in the environment and to early adaptation that may include ramping up options that had previously been nurtured in a low-cost manner.

TASK #3: ORGANIZATIONAL STRUCTURE

Most large firms have a hierarchical command-and-control organizational structure. Top management develops a strategy and orchestrates detailed plans, including budgets with accounting-based performance targets for the firm's business units. The budget represents the marching orders for middle management. This organizational structure originated in the 1920s with General Motors.

Flatter organizational structures are gaining momentum worldwide. Employees at lower levels gain decision-making power over resources and motivation to create value as opposed to doing whatever it takes to hit accounting targets. A noteworthy example in the steel industry is Nucor. Ken Iverson was CEO of Nucor from 1965 to 1996 and developed a knowledge-building culture with minimal managerial layers. Nucor has a long-term record of top-notch performance while delivering exceptional compensation to team members based on team performance. In his autobiography, Iverson noted a key ingredient to his worldview:

> The great and terrible irony of modern business is that so many managers feel overburdened with responsibility, while so many employees feel unchallenged and unfulfilled in their jobs. . . . Instead of telling people what to do and then hounding them to do it, our managers focus on *shaping an environment that frees employees to determine what they can do and should do, to the benefit of themselves and the business.*[16] (italics added)

Nucor has delivered continuous innovation, including early adoption of electric arc furnaces that use recycled steel, and has started producing at scale steel with net zero greenhouse gas emissions.

Gary Hamel is a well-known thought leader in business and has authored many influential books. Hamel's partner in the Management

Lab is Michele Zaini. In their book, *Humanocracy: Creating Organizations as Amazing as the People Inside Them*, Hamel and Zaini emphasize:

> What's needed are radically new organizational models that downplay formal structure. In a world of relentless change, trade-offs need to be made as close to the front lines as possible. Boundaries must be malleable. Resources, rather than being hoarded, must flow unhindered toward promising opportunities. Interunit coordination must be the product of nimble, self-organizing communities and market-like transactions . . .
>
> Nucor's model isn't about pushing employees to *do* more, but in giving them the opportunity to *be* more—more than blue-collar workers, more than order takers, more than mere operators, more than employees. Nucor's frontline team members are experts, innovators, risk takers, and owners. Nucor proves unequivocally that *every* job can be a good job, whatever the industry.[17] (Italics in original)

How to transform bureaucratic, slow-moving large firms to nimble, opportunistic firms with employees at all levels equipped and motivated to be value creators? In addition, how to sustain nimble, opportunistic small firms in order to avoid becoming bureaucratic large firms with employees that have the humanity (creativity) sucked out of them? Important questions, right?

Let's consider a creative answer to both questions that originated in Scandinavia. It has produced stellar results for a long list of large European firms by reducing bureaucracy.

The approach is called Beyond Budgeting and is explained in a 2023 book, *This Is Beyond Budgeting: A Guide to More Adaptive and Human Organizations*, authored by Bjarte Bogsnes. The core idea is both simple and powerful: eliminate the budget, which is the heartbeat of command-and-control bureaucracy.

Management (and boards of directors) responsible for large command-and-control firms assume that if top management enabled lower-level employees to make significant resource allocation decisions, this loss of management's power would be detrimental to firm performance. Another unspoken elephant in the room is when management and boards assume that there is no problem when budgets combine the objectives of targets, forecasts, and resource allocations into a single quantitative tool. In my opinion, Bogsnes is on solid ground in arguing for separating these three purposes, thereby allowing for different numbers depending on the purpose. I like his language improvements:

> A target is an *aspiration*, what we want to happen. A forecast is an *expectation*, what we think will happen, whether we like what we see or not. And resource allocation is about *optimization* of scare resources.
>
> . . . Some tell me it is impossible to operate without a budget. My response is that this separation lets us do everything the budget tried to do for us, but now in much better ways: better targets, better forecasts, and a more effective resource allocation. It also improves how we measure, evaluate, reward, and coordinate. How impossible and how scary is that?[18]

The fundamental reasons for improvement are no secret. The conventional budgeting process incentivizes people to lie in order to lower targets making a performance bonus easier to achieve.[19] And forecasting is about painting a rosy picture of a future consistent with allocating more resources to the forecaster's business unit. In addition, budgets do not encourage cost-conscious behavior; rather, if it is in the budget, it is my money to spend. Contrast this with Nucor's management system that enables frontline employees with the best knowledge to decide how to optimize the firm's resources.

Hamel and Zanini in their *Humanocracy* tell a revealing story about Nucor's knowledge-building culture. Members of one of Nucor's teams operating the Blytheville, Arkansas, plant decided, after doing a cost-benefit analysis, that the furnace shell needed to be replaced. Instead of a purchasing department handling this task, the team coordinated bids from suppliers. Dissatisfied and acting like owners, not blue-collar employees, they designed a shell and worked with the fabricator at every step. The new furnace shell was highly efficient and cost $3 million versus the $30 million cost associated with the original bid prices. This story echoes Iverson's point about enabling employees ". . . to determine what they can do and should do, to the benefit of themselves and the business."

In conclusion, after writing this section, I found myself imagining a future in which business school professors begin their accounting class by announcing: "You will learn the mechanics of accounting budgets, but importantly, you will learn why conventional command-and-control budgets are counterproductive, along with ideas for improving the situation."

TASK #4: EFFICIENCY OF EXISTING BUSINESSES

I believe that a prerequisite for a firm to excel at continual gains in efficiency is a knowledge-building culture that equips and motivates people to excel at seeing and solving problems that matter. Let's take a ride around the Knowledge Building Loop to illustrate how important recommendations in the literature about improvements in process, quality, and overall efficiency fit neatly together with the loop components.

Knowledge Base

- Top management knows and supports an environment that treats all employees as value creators. Consequently, employees are mentored to improve their problem skills without being distracted by managers who stroke their own egos by quickly imposing their fix for a problem or directing work-arounds.
- Problem solvers know that the use of systems thinking or linear cause-and-effect thinking depends on the context.

Purposes

- Efficiency is improved by continually reducing (eliminating) waste.
- Waste is any activity that does not add value to what is delivered to customers.

Worldview

- Products or services delivered to customers are produced via value streams, which entail all the actions (including the use of data) during the process of delivering value to customers.
- Systems have a key constraint (bottleneck) that offers the maximum leverage for expeditiously improving the overall system performance by fixing this constraint.

Perceptions

- Work is observed being done in the context of a process that needs to be controlled in order to achieve acceptable variation and high quality.
- Out-of-control situations are learning opportunities.
- Observing firsthand both problems and the results of change (experiments) is more useful than the data in written reports.

- Performance scorecards are ideally displayed as visual guides to help those doing the work to improve.

Actions and Consequences

- Analyze problems deeply, with an eye on interrelationships, and discover root causes so that implementation of a logically sound action plan will eliminate the problem.
- Select some experiments that warrant the involvement of higher levels of management. Then the results of these experiments, if favorable, can not only lead to new useful knowledge for solving immediate problems but also may lead to additional value-creation opportunities.

Feedback

- Keep in mind that accounting-based efficiency measures become more useful at higher levels of the firm and should not be forced on employees at lower levels who need data that directly connects to improving how work gets done.
- Monitor the external environment in order to quickly adapt to change that impacts a firm's operations. Firms participate with other firms (e.g., suppliers) in delivering value to customers. This offers opportunities to join, or lead, an ecosystem that works to the mutual benefit of members and ultimately to the benefit of the final customers (e.g., Apple's App Store). Put on your thinking systems hat.

The above best practices touch on many issues central to lean thinking. Jim Womack and Dan Jones have led the lean thinking revolution in management thinking, which regrettably is not nearly as widespread as it deserves.[20] Womack and Jones conclude that lean thinking is about gaining clarity as to the customer value experience; specifying value streams for each product; organizing for value to flow throughout production via a pull (not push) orientation tied to customer demand; and pursuing perfection.

Jim Womack transitioned from academic work to a specialized "practitioner" deeply immersed in generating practical value-creation insights. He is well known for his gemba walks. *Gemba* is Japanese for where the work gets done. His walks involve the lean tradition of "Go see, ask why, and show respect." Womack made an insightful assessment in the introduction to his book *Gemba Walks*:

> I labored in the university world where it seemed natural to learn by gathering data at arm's length and then evaluating it in an office through the lens of theory. Now I work in an opposite manner by verifying reality on the gemba and using this understanding to create hypotheses for testing about how things can work better.
>
> . . . My purpose in taking a walk is simple: to see and to understand how more value can be created with less waste. But what is the purpose of the value stream along which I'm walking? That is, just what "value" should it provide for its customers? This is a critical question for the lean thinker because diving in to "fix" a process (a value stream) so it can provide more of the wrong "value" can only be an exercise in frustration. Yet I find that many lean practitioners seem hardly aware of the issue.
>
> Once purpose is understood, it's easy to proceed to the more familiar questions of how to create the best process for achieving that purpose and how to creatively engage people in implementing, operating, and improving this process. But purpose comes first.[21]

The importance of how customers experience value cannot be overstated and is central to the next section.

TASK #5: INNOVATION FOR EXISTING AND FUTURE BUSINESSES

The discussion above noted the importance of clarity about the purpose of a value stream to deliver not just a product but a value experience to customers.[22] Why focus on improving the efficiency of manufacturing screws, for example, if the screws add zero value in the eyes of customers and can easily be purchased and not manufactured?

In this section, I discuss innovation that may immediately elicit thoughts about inventing new things. However, let's start by positioning innovation as a means to deliver a value experience. Starbucks did not create anything fundamentally new. Rather, Starbucks provided a place, between home and work, for drinking coffee and socializing—an enjoyable experience.

Let's step back and imagine that we work for a firm with a stellar record for innovation and an enviable knowledge-building culture. What would that be like? First and foremost, there is no fear.[23] People are trusted to experiment, fail and learn, and succeed with the participation of others. The firm is in a constant state of flux because we embrace change and the attendant problems that accompany uncertainty. We know how to build the knowledge needed to turn problems into opportunities. Such a description is not a new idea. Others have studied firms with especially viable cultures and reached a similar conclusion. For example, Mike Rother, a leading expert on Toyota's way of organizing factory work, made an astute observation (note that *kata* is a Japanese term for a way of thinking and behaving):

> Toyota's improvement kata involves teaching people a standardized conscious "means" for sensing the gist of

situations and responding scientifically. This is a different way for humans to have a sense of security, comfort, and confidence. Instead of obtaining that from an unrealistic sense of certainty about conditions, they get it from the means by which they deal with uncertainty. This channels and taps our capabilities as humans much better than our current [modern] management approach, explains a good deal of Toyota's success, and gives us a model for managing almost any human enterprise.[24]

Readers may recognize that I am pitching the Thinking and Doing System of Figure 2.2 as a *generalized* approach to knowledge building and therefore value creation. As a generalized approach, it travels well. It is at the heart of my Pragmatic Theory of the Firm that provides insights to improve decision-making by boards of directors, management, and investors. The Thinking and Doing System spotlights three lessons: (1) making systems thinking an automatic part of how we think, (2) focusing on language, specifically the assumptions behind the words, and (3) asking better questions. This approach works well as a lens to see better how innovation efforts succeed or fail.

Let's take a look at a comprehensive eight-year study by professors Jeff Dyer, Hal Gregerson, and Clayton Christensen that targeted a root-cause explanation for highly significant innovation success. They initially interviewed approximately one hundred well-known, highly successful innovators (e.g., Jeff Bezos) followed by self-reported data for approximately five hundred innovators and more than five thousand executives covering seventy-five countries. They explain their findings in the book *The Innovator's DNA: Mastering the Five Skills of Disruptive Innovators.* The quote below summarizes their findings and reflects fast and effective traversing of the Knowledge Building Loop. In the authors' words:

Five primary discovery skills—skills that compose what we call

> the *innovator's DNA*—surfaced from our conversations. [1] We found that innovators "Think Different," to use a classic Apple slogan. Their minds excel at linking together ideas that aren't obviously related to produce original ideas (we call this cognitive skill "associational thinking" or "associating"). But to think different, innovators had to "act different." [2] All were questioners, frequently asking questions that punctured the status quo. [3] Some observed the world with intensity beyond the ordinary. [4] Others networked with the most diverse people on the face of the earth. [5] Still others placed experimentation at the center of their innovative activity. When engaged in consistently, these actions—questioning, observing, networking, and experimenting—triggered associational thinking to deliver new businesses, products, services, and/or processes. . . . *If we change our behaviors, we can improve our creative impact.*[25] (italics in original)

It should be revealing to compare how innovation thought leaders have different recipes to achieve significant innovation success. When Curtis Carlson was CEO of SRI International, he guided the conception and development of HDTV, Siri, the computer mouse, electronic banking, robotic surgery that evolved into Intuitive Surgical (the dominant robotics surgical firm with its da Vinci system), and much more.

He recommends a structured process grounded in five fundamental elements of active learning:[26]

1. *Iteration with real-time feedback* that ideally achieves one or two insights about the customer experience.
2. *Concise mental models* that, due to their reliability, become part of the innovator's knowledge base.
3. *Multiple learning styles* that resonate with Mike Jackson's

encouragement to adopt systems thinking with its multiple ways of framing and designing solutions to complex problems.

4. *Teamwork* wherein teams of approximately five people share a vision and bring complementary skills and different ways of perceiving the world.
5. *Frequent comparisons* of what team members think they know, which is in the spirit of designing prototypes.

Carlson emphasizes the need for a sound value proposition that requires not being stuck to your favorite idea as the preferred approach. Early on, before building the offering, reduce the major risks associated with a value proposition. To facilitate effective criticism and comparison to alternatives, all value propositions need a common denominator showcasing need, approach, benefits relative to costs, and competition.

Should your firm adopt the way of thinking promoted by Dyer, Gregerson, and Christensen or go with Carlson? This is a good example of asking the wrong question. A better question is: How can your firm modify its innovation approach after a thorough study of both the former and the latter. Furthermore, at the risk of being overly repetitive, viewing both approaches through the lens of the Knowledge Building Loop shows them to be complementary.

How does innovation impact stock prices? Dyer, Gregerson, and Christensen utilized the HOLT % Future for quantifying the proportion of a firm's total market value due to expectations (implied in stock prices) of the value of the firm's future investments. Expectations of economic returns above the cost of capital result in a positive % Future and vice versa. I developed the % Future and it was introduced in my 1999 book, *CFROI Valuation: A Total System Approach to Valuing the Firm*. For many years, both *Forbes* and *Barrons* have utilized % Future to rank firms on innovation skill. This ties back to the life-cycle framework covered in chapter 1. Knowledge building and value creation are opposite sides of the same coin.

TASK #6: CONTEXT-SPECIFIC PERFORMANCE MEASUREMENT

In this section, I explain the key ideas behind context-specific performance measurement. I'll begin with two stories.

John Coyle is an Olympic medalist in speed skating and an expert in design thinking, which closely parallels the Knowledge Building Loop process. His was a tough journey that began at the U.S. Olympic training center. His oxygen capacity test score put him way below anyone else on the team. His maximum power test was equally dismal. However, his anaerobic output (muscular strength for short bursts) was way above others.[27]

Coaches told Coyle that he must improve his weaknesses in preparation for the upcoming U.S. Olympic trials. He totally committed to this conventional advice. His performance steadily worsened, culminating with an abysmal performance at the Olympic trials. Coyle then reframed the problem of how to win. (Note that these races take place in an ice rink with short tracks and ultra-tight curved corners. And cutting corners more tightly is both super dangerous and extremely difficult.) Coyle had the determination, coupled to his unique ability for short bursts of energy, to learn how to routinely and safely execute ultra-tight corners. By doing this throughout the race, he could win by traveling a shorter distance than his competitors. He won a silver medal in the 1994 Olympic winter games.

After transitioning his training to optimize his new approach, he arrived for the 1995 U.S. World Team trials and promptly was hit with the flu. Nevertheless, he recorded superlative performance starting with unofficially breaking the world record in his first race. During the remainder of the competition, he broke every U.S. record in the events in which he competed. Later that year, he skated the fastest time in the world in the 500-meter race at the world championships. Unfortunately, he failed to make the Olympic team due to crashes in the final events.

John Coyle's journey suggests that conventional thinking about performance metrics may be unsuited to the unique capabilities and handicaps of a particular business unit. Context matters. Highly specialized skills that initially don't seem important may provide opportunities to creatively reframe how to win in delivering superb customer experiences (and also secure competitive advantage). Based on his experiences, he recommends accepting your weaknesses, recognizing your particular strengths, reframing the winning problem in the context of your strengths, and doubling down on your strengths.

The second story begins with Debra Smith, a consultant who worked for many years with Eli Goldratt. She strongly advocates locating the system's key impeding-performance constraint and then devoting all efforts to fixing the constraint. The key constraint for one of her clients was a complicated machine that suffered frequent breakdowns. The maintenance employees were measured by a conventional metric: the turnaround time for getting the machine back in operation after a breakdown. Smith had discussions with those doing the work and reached agreement that performance should be measured by how long the machine stayed in operation after a maintenance fix.[28] Everything changed. Maintenance employees now worked on finding root causes of problems and devising logically sound solutions. By eliminating a faulty performance metric (the actual key constraint), employees gained satisfaction from purposeful work that improved overall system performance.

Let's continue with the idea that innovation in performance measurement is a viable approach for improving overall system performance.

Jim Womack and Dan Jones, the thought leaders of the Lean Movement, pose a question about the conventional thinking that utilizes inventory turns and customer complaints:

> . . . How do inventory turns, as a proxy for flow, or customer complaints, as a proxy for product quality, improve performance? In particular, how are these metrics going to improve performance when employees can't see the consumer (who is one or more firms away), can't see the consumption and provision processes (which run across many functions and departments), and have no principles to guide improvement?
>
> . . . What's missing in most organizations is a "chief process officer"—someone at the top who can employ [systems] thinking to take responsibility for the definition and continuous improvement of the key value-creating processes. This means working backward from the customer's complete specification of value.[29]

Womack and Jones see inventory turns and customer complaints as signals that lack meaning for employees to devise actions that can generate desired performance consequences. The key constraint lies in the firm's organizational structure that lacks a chief process officer. Debra Smith began with how maintenance employees perceived the task at hand, and she changed those perceptions to achieve performance not otherwise available. And John Coyle achieved breakthrough performance by asking penetrating questions that overturned the "knowledge" of expert coaches and creatively reframed the problem of winning to shortening the distance he skated versus competitors. These examples illustrate that progress ultimately depends on effectively traversing the Knowledge Building Loop. I'll add one more example based on personal experience where attention to perception, language, and related loop thinking led the Patent Office to issue multiple patents for a potential disruptive invention. This example will be more meaningful for readers who have online brokerage accounts and trade stocks.

My Liquidity Builder is a novel way to more efficiently trade securities. I began by asking a question: What does best price mean? The brokerage industry says that best price for a buy order is a trade slightly lower than the current ask quote and for a sell order slightly above the bid quote. They call it price improvement. The flip side is that your limit order to buy or sell sits unexecuted as market-makers jump ahead of you and often trade a few tenths of a cent ahead of your limit order. Market-makers like Citadel are hugely profitable, and they pay brokerage firms for routing your order to them for execution. It is called payment for order flow.

In contrast, I define best price to include the time to execute your entire order at a price close to the midpoint of the current bid-ask spread. One of the many claims covered in my patents is for limit orders based not on the time the order was entered but on the order size. With the Liquidity Builder, retail investors with big orders to fill can connect with institutional investors and quickly execute their order and save literally days of time versus the status quo and trade close to the midpoint of the bid-ask spread to the mutual benefit of each party. In conversations with leaders in the brokerage industry and exchanges, I was told that the Liquidity Builder would work. However, by obsoleting payment for order flow while delivering better prices (properly defined), the Liquidity Builder disrupts the industry profit model. Keep in mind that significant cash commissions for Liquidity Builder trades could be utilized because of the value received by participants. The patents have exceptionally broad claims and cover any type of securities. I have so far been unable to implement this invention at scale via a large brokerage firm and/or an exchange.

Conclusion

Curiosity, humility, and questioning about what you think you know all promote effective traversing of the Knowledge Building Loop. As does critiquing the language you use (especially its unarticulated assumptions), along with playful but serious imagination for connecting things and seeking different ways of perceiving problems. The lesson: think more about how you think using the components of the Knowledge Building Loop as guideposts for reassessing how, for example, your worldview constrains your formulation of a problem and the data selected to assess actions and consequences. This reassessment can reveal new connections among the key interrelated managerial tasks that, in turn, will lead to better questions and novel, useful ideas.

The above discussion of the six critical managerial tasks suggests that whatever one's position in an organization's hierarchy, benefits accrue from building knowledge that improves one's performance and in helping others do the same. In this regard, I have had many experiences exchanging my ideas and learning about the ideas of my colleagues in the network that I have built up, including:

- I learned about the different levels of systems thinking expertise needed by management from Mark van Clieaf, coauthor of *Net Zero Business Models: Winning in the Global Net Zero Economy.* This book contains an extensive analysis of how the life-cycle framework can guide management's strategy to choose the appropriate pathway to net zero, such as this chapter 11 excerpt:

  > A board of directors should have a measurement and reporting process for return on capital, cost of capital, economic profit, and future value [% Future] to guide effective allocation policies and strategies. Bartley Madden's . . . life-cycle framework will not only help companies to choose the appropriate

> pathway to net zero but also provides a tool that boards can use to monitor, preserve, and enhance shareholder value.

- On a regular basis, I was invited by Professor Mark Frigo to present topics related to knowledge building and value creation to his MBA students at the Center for Strategy, Execution and Valuation at DePaul University. Through interactions with Mark, I gained insights on packaging and marketing my ideas to practitioners and academics. One such idea is a Life Cycle Review of the firm's business units to help board members fulfill their responsibilities. Mark and I explained this idea in a St*rategic Finance* article—"Strategic Life-Cycle Analysis: The Role of the CFO."
- David Koenig is one of the top corporate governance thought leaders, and we have had productive conversations as part of his DCRO Institute, which is the leading source of risk governance training and credentialing. He concurs with my definition of firm risk as obstacles to achieving the firm's purpose. Koenig expands on my concept of firm risk in his book *The Board Member's Guide to Risk*, which also explains the key ideas in my Pragmatic Theory of the Firm, including this excerpt from chapter 8:

  > Madden's research was quite successful and yielded a concept now known as corporate "fade." [See life-cycle figure in chapter 1.] It's a clever term to describe the common tendency of firms to see a [decline] of their excess returns over the cost of capital as they mature. . . . Fade reflects a lack of innovation. . . . Fade can be beaten through

> a process that Madden refers to as *knowledge-building proficiency*. His is a systems approach to understanding how organizations work, and has led him to the creation of . . . the Pragmatic Theory of the Firm. (italics in original)

There are two primary punchlines for this chapter. First, in general, the Knowledge Building Loop of Figure 2.1 can help a wide audience of problem solvers because it facilitates insightful answers to better questions. In particular, it is an especially useful foundation for management and for those aspiring to join the managerial ranks. Second, the Thinking and Doing System of Figure 2.2 promotes new angles of thinking that can improve performance with the six critical managerial tasks and comports very well with Larry Smarr's vision for remaking the university. For example, Smarr, one of the world's leading scientists, wrote:

> If you look at any university, the reward structure is entirely based on single-warrior combat. But if you want to attack the real-world problems that we face, it's a team sport, with specialists in many different fields. We've had a century of reductionism, but at some point, you need to put all of that knowledge back together in a synthesis.[30]

Now is the time to do it.

The next chapter describes how my Pragmatic Theory of the Firm delivers insights about the role of capitalism in promoting economic progress. Academic theories of the firm invariably focus on only one aspect of the firm (e.g., the resource-based theory of the firm focuses on developing and utilizing resources). But how can management improve resource-allocation decisions? This returns full circle to the preeminence of a firm's knowledge-building proficiency. And, in addition, we need a theory of the firm that recognizes and encourages this basic fact, not only to illuminate the way forward for managers but also to redirect away from the silo-based thinking.

NOTES

[1] Edward D. Hess. 2014. *Learn or Die: Using Science to Build a Leading-Edge Organization.* New York: Columbia University Press. p. 75.

[2] Eric Beinhocker and Nick Hanauer. September 1, 2014. "Redefining capitalism." *McKinsey Quarterly.* For an overview of the shortcomings of neoclassical economics and its treatment of the firm, see Chapter 1 of *Value Creation Principles.*

[3] Bartley J. Madden. 2012. "Management's Worldview: Four Critical Points about Reality, Language, and Knowledge Building to Improve Organizational Performance." *Journal of Organizational Computing and Electronic Commerce* 22(4): 334-346.

[4] Teppo Felin. July 5, 2018. "The fallacy of obviousness." *Aeon Essays.* https://aeon.co/essays/are-humans-really-blind-to-the-gorilla-on-the-basketball-court.

[5] William H. Starbuck. 2006. *The Production of Knowledge: The Challenge of Social Science Research.* Oxford: Oxford University Press. pp. 16-18.

[6] Michael C. Jackson. 2019. *Critical Systems Thinking and the Management of Complexity.* Hoboken, NJ: John Wiley & Sons p. xix.

[7] John Seddon, 2019. *Beyond Command and Control.* London: Mayfield Press.

[8] John Seddon. 2003. *Freedom from Command & Control: A better way to make the work work.* Buckingham, UK: Vanguard Education Ltd. p. 168.

[9] Rodger L. Martin. "My Eureka Moment with Strategy." May 3, 2010. *Harvard Business Review.*

[10] Hal Gregersen. 2018. *Questions Are the Answer: A Breakthrough Approach to Your Most Vexing Problems at Work and in Life.* New York: HarperCollins. p. 29.

[11] Edgar H. Schein. 2010. 4th ed. *Organizational Culture and Leadership.* San Franciso: Jossey-Bass. p. 18.

[12] Edgar H. Schein. pp. 369-371

[13] Amy Y. Ou, David A. Waldman, and Suzane J. Peterson. 2018. "Do Humble CEOs Matter? An Examination of CEO Humility and Firm Outcomes." *Journal of Management.* 44(3): 1147-1173.

[14] Interview. April 16, 2008. "Bezos on Innovation." *Bloomberg Businessweek.*

[15] Richard P. Rumelt. 2022. *The Crux: How Leaders Become Strategists.* New York: PublicAffairs. p. 292.

[16] Ken Iverson. 1998. *Plain Talk: Lessons from a Business Maverick.* Hoboken, NJ: John Wiley & Sons. p. 98.

[17] Gary Hamel and Michele Zanini. 2020. *Humanocracy: Creating Organizations as Amazing as the People Inside Them.* Boston, MA: Harvard Business Review Press. p. 31 and 82-83.

[18] Bjarte Bogsnes. 2023. *This Is Beyond Budgeting: A Guide to More Adaptive and Human Organizations*. Hoboken, NJ: John Wiley & Sons. pp. 36-37.

[19] Michael C. Jensen. 2003. "Paying People to Lie: The Truth about the Budgeting Process." *European Financial Management*. 9(3): 379-406.

[20] Womack and Jones coauthored the two classic lean thinking books *The Machine That Changed the World* (Dan Roos was also a coauthor) and *Lean Thinking: Banish Waste and Create Wealth in Your Corporation*.

[21] Jim Womack. 2nd edition. 2013. *Gemba Walks*. Cambridge, MA: Lean Enterprise Institute. pp. xix and 1.

[22] Mark Packard. 2022. *Entrepreneurial Valuation: An Entrepreneur's Guide to Getting into the Minds of Customers*. Berlin, Germany: De Gruyter.

[23] Amy Edmondson. *The Fearless Organization: Creating Psychological Safety in the Workplace for Learning, Innovation, and Growth*. Hoboken, NJ: John Wiley & Sons.

[24] Mike Rother. 2010. *Toyota Kata: Managing People for Improvement, Adaptiveness, and Superior Results*. New York: McGraw Hill. p. 165.

[25] Jeff Dyer, Hal Gregersen, and Clayton M. Christensen. 2019. *The Innovator's DNA: Mastering the Five Skills of Disruptive Innovator*s. Boston, MA. Harvard Business Review Press. p. 3.

[26] Curtis R. Carlson. 2020. "Innovation for Impact." *Harvard Business Review*. November-December.

[27] John K. Coyle. 2018. "Design for your Strengths." *Strategy+Business*. Spring issue (90).

[28] Debra Smith. 2000. *The Measurement Nightmare: How the Theory of Constraints Can Resolve Conflicting Strategies, Policies, and Measures*. New York: St. Lucie Press. p. 14.

[29] James P. Womack and Daniel T. Jones. 2005. *Lean Solutions: How Companies and Customers Can Create Value and Wealth Together*. New York: Free Press. p. 177.

[30] Lawrence M. Fisher. October 9, 2017. "Why Larry Smarr Is Pioneering Collaborative Innovation." *Strategy+Business*. Winter issue (89).

CHAPTER 3

Capitalism and Society[1]

UNDERSTANDING THE BENEFITS OF CAPITALISM THROUGH THE LENS OF A NEW THEORY OF THE FIRM

Bartley J. Madden

Introduction

Focusing on the performance of firms promotes a bottom-up approach to understanding the benefits of capitalism. In contrast, capitalism's critics (Chalmers 2022; Mazzucato 2021) contend that it promotes maximizing shareholder value and related short-termism to the detriment of all of a firm's stakeholders and that only a big government fix can address issues such as inequality and climate change. This paper answers a call for a counter argument (Klein et al. 2022) to capitalism's critics by exploring how the Pragmatic Theory of the Firm (Madden 2020, 2021) provides insights about how knowledge building at the firm level translates into progress at the macro level (standard of living).

Section 1 lays the foundation of this paper by explaining how firms build knowledge and create value. These are two sides of the same coin and fundamental to how a firm operates and survives. Section 2 introduces the Knowledge Building Loop to clarify and delineate the knowledge-building process, thereby laying the groundwork for how to nurture and sustain a knowledge-building culture. Section 3 introduces the Pragmatic Theory, which offers a four-part purpose of the firm and positions maximizing shareholder value not as the purpose of the firm but as the result of a firm successfully achieving its four-part purpose. Moreover, knowledge-building proficiency relative to competitors is viewed as the critical determinant of a firm's long-term performance. Building on the previous sections, section 4 explains shortcomings of corporate governance (boards of directors) and proposes a solution. Section 5 highlights the main takeaways from this paper.

Capitalism, knowledge building, and value creation

Capitalism is usefully defined as "a system in which (1) factors of production are (mostly) privately owned, (2) resources are (mostly) allocated through markets, and (3) individuals and groups are (mostly) free to engage in economic activity without centralized control or interference from the state" (Klein et al. 2022, 8).

Economic progress under capitalism is achieved when firms (small or large) or individual inventors or entrepreneurs solve formidable problems that eventually spawn large-scale job creation. No less important is a firm's problem-solving activities that reduce waste (efficiency gains) and develop new product or service advancements in delivering value to customers (innovation gains; Garud et al. 2013; Henderson 2021).

Value creation is the design, production, and delivery of a product or service at an affordable price so that the overall customer experience after using the product says: "This is a good deal." Firms can create value for customers via efficiency that enables an affordable price and through innovation that upgrades the customer experience to a new superior level. The bottom line is that economic progress mirrors value created for customers (Packard 2022).

Capitalism enables dynamism: actively seeking new experiences, often technology enabled, that can lead to exciting new opportunities. Capitalism also enables working at meaningful jobs that improve problem-solving skills while providing personal satisfaction (Cerasoli et al. 2014); embracing change in the environment that can advance career opportunities; and communicating useful knowledge to those inside and outside the firm (Garicano and Wu 2012).

As to new experiences, consider people living in cities during the era of horse-drawn transportation. City dwellers experienced myriad difficulties with navigating horse-drawn carriages in a crowded environment, and the air they breathed was full of pulverized horse manure. The first significant innovation to better serve urban customers' transportation needs was the electric streetcar, first installed in 1881. However, the next significant innovation—the automobile—eliminated the need for horse-drawn transportation.

In 1891, Henry Ford began work in Detroit as an engineer for the Edison Illuminating Company. Given his expertise with steam engines, Ford was promoted to chief engineer in 1893. Working at night and on weekends, Ford built by hand his first automobile. The 500-pound quadricycle was completed in 1896 and was powered by a gasoline-fueled internal combustion engine (Rhodes 2018).

Ford's vision of a mass market for gasoline-fueled automobiles required many problems to be solved. A key solver was Charles F. Kettering who invented the electric starter and played an important role in the refining of gasoline well suited for internal combustion engines.

Ford developed significant new knowledge as to how to efficiently mass produce automobiles. This was the beginning of lean manufacturing. Big leaps in knowledge building tied to delivering favorable customer experiences have profound implications for living standards. Introduced in 1908, the Model T was the first affordable automobile and ignited large-scale job creation through new business expansions—roads and bridges, restaurants, hotels, sale and servicing of automobiles, gas stations, tires, steel, businesses that manufactured components for automobiles, and the list goes on. This expanded ecosystem of automobile-related businesses supported new transportation experiences, far beyond just urban driving. Competitors geared up to compete against Ford's innovations to the ultimate benefit of customers.

Ford's competitors could hitchhike on his knowledge building. In the 1950s, Taiichi Ohno built upon Henry Ford's ideas thereby laying the groundwork for Toyota to efficiently mass produce automobiles with very high quality in a large selection of different models. This was far removed from the Model T being Ford's only model, with all Model Ts painted black (Ohno [1978] 1988). The resulting Toyota Production System improved the quality of automobiles greatly, and this new Japanese competition forced other automobile manufacturers worldwide to innovate and improve quality.

Moreover, the lean-manufacturing way of thinking and building knowledge has spread worldwide throughout many industries. Knowledge building is critically important because it is the fundamental cause of efficiency gains and innovation.

A firm's knowledge-building proficiency relative to competitors is the key to how a firm progresses over its life cycle. A firm's life cycle evolves as a continual competitive battle to outperform competitors and earn above-average profitability. This competitive process is illustrated by Ford's early competitive advantage being dissipated as General Motors began offering a variety of models and color choices that better addressed customer demand. A firm's success depends upon management's ability to understand change, adapt early, continually build or acquire new capabilities, and sustain a knowledge-building culture.

Knowledge-building proficiency

Our brains have evolved to promote survival and to use past experiences to shape our perceptions of what is "out there" (Barrett 2020, 10). We see what our brains tell us to see. People with much different past experiences see the world differently. When a skilled astronomer looks at the sky at night or a master chess player at an ongoing chess game, they see things most people don't see.

Improving our knowledge base by purging faulty assumptions and adding more useful and reliable assumptions is illustrated by the six-step Knowledge Building Loop (see fig. 1; Madden 2020). Our *knowledge base* is basically an inventory of assumptions, with varying degrees of reliability, about how the world works based on our past experiences. The reliability of linear cause-and-effect analysis applied to nonliving things can produce unwarranted confidence when the same logic is used to analyze complex systems such as human behavior (Powers 1973).

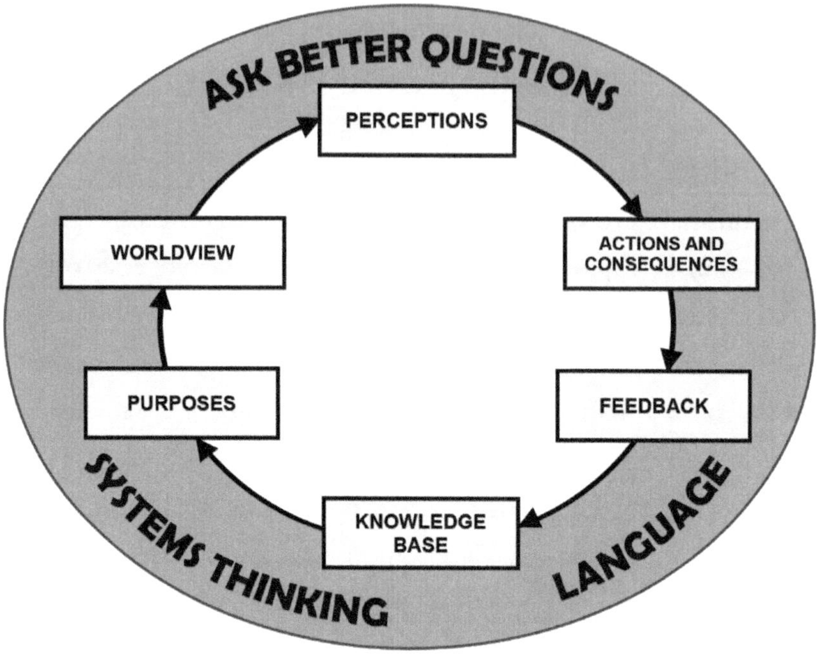

Figure 1. Knowledge Building Loop
Source: The original version of this figure appeared in my 2012 article "Management's Worldview: Four Critical Points about Reality, Language, and Knowledge Building to Improve Organizational Performance."[2]

We observe how people behave, and at times it makes little sense to us. However, if we understand their *purposes*, then their actions are seen as a means to get what they want (Marken and Horth 2011). An especially important component of the Knowledge Building Loop is one's *worldview*, which is the ideas and beliefs by which we interpret and interact with the world. Our worldview influences how we frame problems and develop hypotheses; it affects even the data we select to test hypotheses. Shared worldviews can lead to cooperation, whereas sharply different worldviews can lead to conflict. In dealing with complex problems, it is advantageous to see the world as a systems thinker, that is, one who is keenly aware of relationships among system components and seeks alternative ways of seeing problems that can elucidate previously unrecognized relationships and assumptions that are no longer valid.

When Cisco acquired WebEx, the acquired management's worldview was rooted in its global customers' demand for round-the-clock perfect reliability with high quality for video meetings. In contrast, Cisco management's worldview was attuned to buyers of long-lived equipment (e.g., routers, servers). Frustrated with their failure to get funding to build improved software needed to deliver their vision of a future for video meetings, Eric Yuan and other engineers left Cisco to start Zoom.

We actively shape our *perceptions* of the world (Felin et al. 2017). Is it possible to change how we perceive the world? According to the neuroscientist Beau Lotto (2017, 118–19; italics in the original): "In order to see differently, we must first see *seeing* itself differently. This is important in a deep, lived sense beyond just the visual. . . . Getting a stronger sense of the principles of your own brain allows you to see how subtly past experience not only biases us, but creates us. Knowing this, you can learn to take ownership over your brain's apparatus and thus make *new* pasts that will change your brain's perception of future possibilities."

Note that the language we use promotes an independent reality for things. Assigning names to things encourages linear cause-and-effect thinking. Consider the phrase *accounting costs* in a situation where workstation A in a manufacturing line feeds parts to workstation B, which happens to be the bottleneck (key constraint) in the manufacturing line. By installing a faster machine at A, we then perceive lower accounting costs (improved efficiency) for A. However, our *actions* have caused unintended *consequences* due to a faulty assumption. The faster flowing of parts from A to B worsens the bottleneck at B and degrades overall system performance. The faulty assumption behind the phrase, *accounting costs*, is that components of a system operate independently of one another.

The final component of the Knowledge Building Loop is *feedback*. This can potentially change our knowledge base given what is learned about the consequences of our actions. Overall, figure 1 emphasizes the importance of asking better questions that can change the way we perceive problems and can lead to innovative solutions. Consider the problem of dirty clothes in space. NASA first asked, How can we *get* clothes clean in space? NASA later asked, How can we *keep* clothes clean in space? A better question that led to an innovative approach using clothes with built-in antimicrobials (Shapiro 2020).

Knowledge building results from effective traversing of the Knowledge Building Loop and is enabled by having an open mind, that is, constructive skepticism about what we think we know. Ray Dalio, whose money-management career at Bridgewater Associates was extraordinarily successful, summarizes: "To be radically open-minded you must . . . sincerely believe that you might not know the best possible path and recognize that your ability to deal well with 'not knowing' is more important than whatever it is you do know. . . . Radically open-minded people know that coming up with the *right question* and asking other smart people what they think is as important as having all the answers. . . . What exists within the area of 'not knowing' is so much greater and more exciting than anything any one of us knows" (2017, 188; italics added).

The process of expanding our knowledge base into the area of "not knowing" begins with imagination and asking better questions (Weick 1989). Imagination is about our capacity to form internal images of objects or situations that can result in novel combinations and possibilities of what can be. Imagination helps unframe problems that our worldviews have previously framed due to reliance on assumptions from our knowledge base that we strongly believed to be reliable (Martin 2022). Ann M. Pendleton-Jullian and John Seely Brown (2018, 1:356) make a fundamental point about imagination: "Real world experiences seed rich image banks for the imagination to draw on. . . . We rely on the imagination for adaptability, especially on its propensity for playing with banked images. If the brain were limited merely to retaining experiences unaltered, we would be stuck in the familiar, the stable, and the known, unable to adapt to the new and unexpected in a constantly changing environment. But we do adapt. We process and adjust to an environment where new conditions and experiences abound, and we do so through the imagination."

Does using the Knowledge Building Loop as a guidepost for analyzing innovation initiatives help to better understand innovators' thinking? Answering this question may illuminate how the Knowledge Building Loop leads to insights of practical importance for planning and executing innovation projects. Consider the experience of the Wright brothers.

Over a four-year time span and using revenue from their bicycle shop, Wilbur and Orville Wright successfully developed, and in 1903 were the first to fly, an engine-powered airplane. How best to analyze this remarkable innovation, and more specifically, how best to analyze the Wright brothers' knowledge-building process? The Knowledge Building Loop provides a way of thinking about building knowledge that is foundational to understanding both successful innovations and those that fail.

The six components for building knowledge are expanded in table 1 in order to provide more specificity about delivering innovations that matter, that is, a new world of experiences much appreciated by customers. One might perceive the process outlined in table 1 as simply common sense. However, we typically do not concern ourselves with, for example, how our past experiences shape what we perceive or how our worldview has automatically framed a problem. This is subtle stuff and hence the benefit of the Expanded Knowledge Building Loop. And we would expect those who are expert in traversing the six steps to have had a rigorous formal education or an unusually useful informal education or training.

1. Knowledge Base	Imagine new assumptions that are strikingly different from conventional assumptions and can lead to significantly improved customer experiences.
2. Purposes	Validate new assumptions and identify and solve problems in order to deliver new customer experiences.
3. Worldview	Tentatively accept new assumptions as reliable guideposts, which then impacts the lens you use to see.
4. Perceptions	See more clearly what needs to be different and carefully craft statements of perceived problems.
5. Actions and Consequences	Test the usefulness of the new assumptions and of the proposed solutions to problems.
6. Feedback	Analyze actions and consequences to reassess assumptions in your knowledge base and to formulate better questions.

Table 1. Expanded Knowledge Building Loop

Here we return full circle to the advantages of a knowledge-building culture for firms. The hallmark of successful innovators is a passionate determination to systematically traverse the needed steps in the Knowledge Building Loop in order to solve problems. Let's return to the Wright brothers' story and analyze their thinking using the guideposts in the Expanded Knowledge Building Loop. The beginning point for innovations that matter—the *knowledge base*—is to imagine new assumptions that are *strikingly different from conventional assumptions* and can lead to much-improved customer experiences (air transportation). The extensive correspondence of the Wright brothers (Wright and Wright 2001) plus how they actually organized their work reflect two key differences in their assumptions versus competitors that led the way to the first engine-operated airplane (the Wright Flyer):

- The Wright brothers' primary goal was *control* of the airplane, whereas their competitors' primary goal was *stability*.
- The solutions to problems must be consistent with the airplane being viewed as a *complex system* and support the pilot's ability to control the airplane. The Wright brothers' competitors ignored the pilot's role as an integral part of the system.

The reason the Wright brothers were able to see past the prevailing wisdom is that they had extensive past experience with bicycles, which are inherently unstable until the bicycle rider (the pilot) learns how to operate and control the bicycle. The challenge of control inextricably leads to systems thinking.

Concerning the second step in table 1, *purposes*, the Wright brothers envisioned a series of experiments that would significantly improve upon existing knowledge and provide well-earned confidence that the Wright Flyer would be a success. In an 1899 letter to the Smithsonian Museum, Wilbur wrote, "I wish to avail myself of all that is already known" (quoted in McCullough 2015, 27). Experiments were performed with kites and gliders yielding essential new knowledge in a relatively safe environment. Not so for many pilots who died trying to fly the designs of competitors who were confident in their "big ideas" and ignored the need for system-level experiments.

The brothers shared a *worldview* (step three) that their key assumptions about the paramount importance of control and the usefulness of systems thinking were stakes in the ground that would prove to be reliable guideposts. Their constructive skepticism about what others had done and their own proposed solutions represented a scientific lens for seeing the world. In Orville's words, "We had to go ahead and discover everything ourselves" (quoted in McCullough 2015, 65).

Perceptions (step four) for the Wright brothers were shaped by the recognized need for pilot control. As such, they perceived a problem with the fundamental design of rigid wings that hampered control when flying in a straight line and especially when attempting to turn the airplane. Wilbur, ever on the lookout for ideas to solve problems, played with a long cardboard box. He flexed the box on both ends and changed its cross-sectional shape without causing damage to the box. This suggested to Wilbur that sections of the wings could be moved in opposite directions (referred to as wing warping) in order to restore equilibrium or navigate a turn. This proved to be a breakthrough idea (Bereiter 2009).

As to the fifth step in the Expanded Knowledge Building Loop, *actions and consequences*, the heretofore widely accepted empirical results related to lift and drag on a wing's surface were found to be in serious error. The brothers built a small-scale wind tunnel using a wooden box and a fan. They meticulously constructed miniature wing models and proceeded to run extensive wind-tunnel experiments that yielded far more accurate data. Orville summarized, "Earlier experimenters had so little accurate knowledge concerning the properties of cambered [asymmetry between the two surfaces of an airfoil] surfaces that they used cambered surfaces of great inefficiency, and the tables of air pressures . . . were so erroneous as to entirely mislead them. . . . I believe we possessed in 1902 more data on cambered surfaces . . . a hundred times over, than all of our predecessors put together" (quoted in Jakab 1990, 156).

Feedback (final step) about the detailed data from the wind-tunnel experiments was an important step in achieving powered flight. The wind-tunnel data led to confidence in designing both wings and propellers. The Wright brothers ingeniously viewed a propeller as a wing traveling in a spiral course. As their work culminated in the final construction of the Wright Flyer, both Wilbur and Orville grew ever more confident that their knowledge-building process would yield success where so many others had failed. Shortly after the historic flights on December 17, 1903, in a statement to the Associated Press, the brothers summarized what had happened and affirmed that their primary goal was achieved—so "we . . . packed our goods and returned home, knowing that the age of the flying machine had come at last" (quoted in Jakab 1990, 213). The above analysis, guided by the Expanded Knowledge Building Loop of table 1, illustrates the need for innovators to appreciate the complexity of situations and research deeply enough to understand what problems need to be handled in order to achieve success. Wilbur Wright put it succinctly: "It is the complexity of the flying problem that makes it so difficult. It is not to be solved by stumbling upon a secret, but by the patient accumulation of information upon a hundred different points, some of which an investigator would naturally think it unnecessary to go into deeply. That is why we think a quick solution impossible" (Wright and Wright [1951] 1996, 189).

The Wright brothers' approach to knowledge building made sense in terms of the six steps of the Expanded Knowledge Building Loop and is consistent with a large body of research on entrepreneurship (Kerr et al. 2014). The six steps are grounded in how our brains function and the role of past experiences in shaping how we see the world. This suggests that innovators should take great care in specifying and evaluating the uniqueness and upside potential from the new assumptions they are betting on. And the same extreme care should be afforded to asking better questions related to the specification of problems, proposed solutions, and needed experiments in order to achieve success. This way of thinking challenges the popular lean-startup methodology, which has been insightfully criticized by Felin et al. (2019, 4; italics in the original):

> We view the central limitation of the lean startup as its tendency to orient entrepreneurs toward ideas and products that can *quickly* and transparently be tested with customers. . . .

> Any customer signal will likely lead startups to pivot toward more incremental and obvious opportunities. The most valuable entrepreneurial ideas are those that are *un*likely to permit an easy, immediately-recognizable experiment. They require some kind of contrarian belief, vision about and commitment toward a counterfactual world that may not easily be recognizable by other market actors.

To sum up, the Knowledge Building Loop connects, in a straightforward way, its six components to the knowledge-building process. The loop offers a means to understand the process of knowledge building that is central to the theory of the firm discussed in the next section.

The pragmatic theory of the firm

What is invariably overlooked by critics, and even many supporters of capitalism, is the need for a viable theory of the firm that treats the firm as a holistic system and brings clarity to the purpose of the firm. The Pragmatic Theory of the Firm is one such theory. It is rooted in systems thinking and specifies the following four-part purpose for the firm:

- Communication of a *vision* of the firm and its social as well as economic mission with the power to motivate and even inspire employees.
- *Continuous gains in efficiency and sustained innovation* that enable the firm to provide operating returns that at least equal its cost of capital, which in turn depend on a firm's knowledge-building proficiency. No firm that fails to provide its investors with competitive returns can survive and prosper.
- *Commitment to building and maintaining win-win relationships* with all of the firm's stakeholders.
- *Investment in the well-being of future generations.* Management

and the board should commit the firm to making contributions to the sustainability of the environment, contributions that the firm is well-positioned to carry out. This should be done with particular attention to the design of products and manufacturing processes that aim to minimize waste and pollution, which again depends on a firm's knowledge-building proficiency.

Importantly, the finance principle of maximizing shareholder value is best positioned not as the purpose of the firm but as the result of a firm successfully achieving its purpose. However, this underscores a central message of corporate finance: to survive and prosper requires that a firm earn at least the cost of capital over the long term.

This theory views the firm as a holistic system and, as illustrated in figure 2, focuses on the connectedness among the firm's purpose, its major activities, and its long-term performance. Some of the benefits of the Pragmatic Theory include attention to, and improvements in, analysis of a firm's history and of the value-creation potential of planned capital expenditures; construction of plausible scenarios about future performance; and questions about the assumptions underpinning the firm's strategy as well as the firm's knowledge-building proficiency versus competitors.

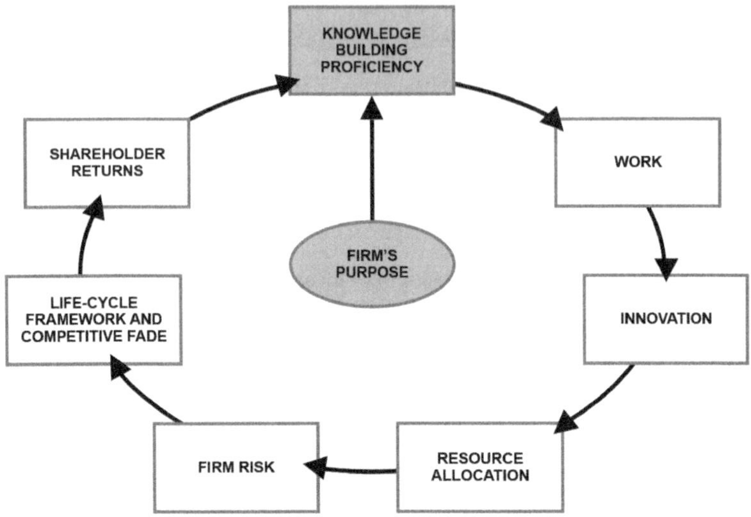

Figure 2. Components of the Pragmatic Theory of the Firm
Source: Madden 2020, 31.

This theory is based on the following tenets as to knowledge building and firm performance:

- Knowledge-building proficiency relative to competitors is the fundamental cause of a firm's long-term performance.
- Improvements in a firm's knowledge-building culture lead to job satisfaction and employee productivity.
- A firm's organizational structure and its culture are closely connected and impact work, innovation, and resource allocation.
- Firm risk is about the obstacles that management faces which interfere with achieving the firm's four-part purpose, for example, a willingness to condone whatever it takes to meet accounting targets.
- A firm's performance—distilled into long-term life-cycle track records of economic returns and reinvestment rates—is a far more insightful lens compared to earnings per share growth rates and is especially useful for resource allocation decisions.

Excess positive or negative shareholder returns over the long term are caused by life-cycle performance greater or less than investor expectations at the beginning of the period (Madden 2020, 150–53). Stated differently, managements and boards should identify their firm's life-cycle stage and then focus on the related key managerial task in order to generate favorable fade of economic returns and reinvestment rates, which is illustrated more fully in figure 3.

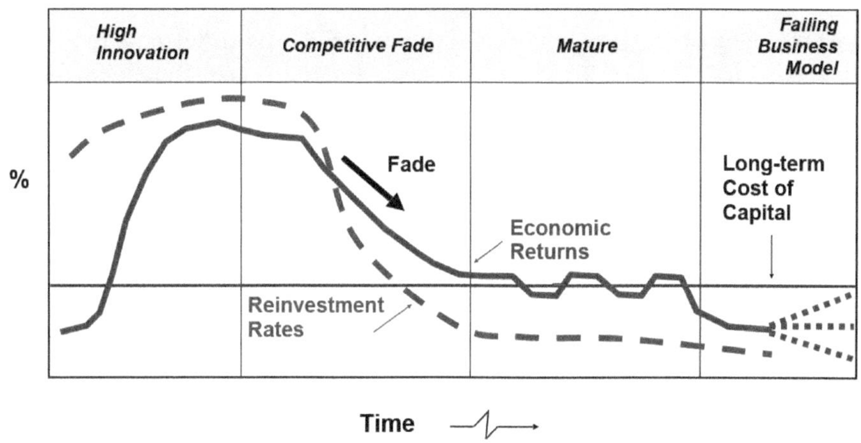

Figure 3. The Life-Cycle Framework

Figure 3 shows a firm's life-cycle stages reflecting the dynamics of a firm's profitability and growth. At the *high-innovation stage,* the key task is to quickly confirm or refute the startup's core business-model assumptions. Economic returns (returns on capital) well above the cost of capital indicate successful commercialization. High and sustained reinvestment rates typically indicate a business that can scale.

Competitors try to duplicate and improve upon the firm's business model, especially when high reinvestment rates suggest a big market opportunity.

At the *competitive fade* stage, economic returns fade toward the cost of capital and reinvestment rates (organic growth) fade toward a much slower growth rate. Management that delivers a favorable fade of economic returns most often has a well-functioning knowledge-building culture and win-win partnerships with all stakeholders. In particular, management needs continually to build or acquire new capabilities to stay a step ahead of competitors.

Eventually, the firm enters the *mature* stage and delivers cost-of-capital returns with slow growth rates. Management needs to adapt early to change in the environment and the key task is to simultaneously improve the efficiency of existing businesses that pay the bills and innovate in new areas, possibly in competition with existing businesses. No easy task.

Sustained below-cost-of-capital economic returns coupled to a business-as-usual culture is the hallmark of the *failing business-model* stage. The top priority is to purge the business-as-usual culture and implement a restructuring plan that may entail hiring a new CEO and the replacement of some board members.

The life-cycle framework coupled to the life-cycle valuation model and global database has a long history of use by money-management organizations (Holland and Matthews 2018) and corporate consultants (Frigo and Madden 2020). The framework focuses on a firm's long-term performance and quantifies competitive advantage via the fade rate. Systems thinking (Jackson 2019) is essential in analyzing the interplay of context and skill in causing long-term financial performance packaged as a life-cycle track record. Organizational structure, culture, strategy, R&D, and resource allocation are connected components of a system that ideally is targeted to achieving the firm's four-part purpose, which is the primary responsibility for the board of directors.

As managers rise in the corporate hierarchy, the more important becomes their systems-thinking skill. The importance of this skill is emphasized by Paul Polman (2014), who had an exceptional track record as CEO of Unilever:

> I truly believe that future leaders will be systems thinkers. It is inconceivable that anyone will successfully steer companies, or countries, through our volatile world without understanding the inter-dependencies between the systems on which we depend.

Corporate governance upgrade

The foregoing discussion leads to two ideas for upgrading corporate governance that deserve attention. First, board members should actively engage with a viable theory of the firm, such as the Pragmatic Theory. The connectedness integral to this theory brings a way of seeing (and thinking) that leads to asking better questions, which may reveal obsolete assumptions. This theory provides a reasoned argument for focusing decision-making on long-term value creation and, in the same spirit, breaking the hold of Wall Street's hyper focus on quarterly results.

A sharpened lens for seeing connections encourages board members to embrace systems thinking. Currently, a particularly critical challenge for a board is to jointly develop with management a workable plan to achieve their firm's net-zero (carbon-emissions) goals. In the forthcoming book, *Net Zero Business Models: Winning in the Global Net Zero Economy,* John Montgomery and Mark Van Clieaf (2023) utilize systems thinking to guide a comprehensive analysis of what it takes to develop such a plan. Their analysis includes a firm's current life-cycle stage (fig. 3), which has major implications for a firm's net-zero transition. Should the board rely solely on popular ESG metrics attuned to carbon emissions as guideposts? Many stakeholder groups, along with Wall Street analysts, believe so. However, there is a strong case, based on systems thinking, that these ESG metrics ignore the most important tool in achieving net zero: firms' committing their innovation efforts to research and designing new products and services to help their customers reduce their carbon emissions (Madden 2023). For example, General Motors was the first customer to sign up for Nucor's latest innovative product—the world's first net-zero carbon steel.

Second, institutional shareholders (especially pension funds and sovereign wealth funds with long-term horizons) are in the best position to orchestrate changes in the selection process for new board members. On the one hand, the preference is for all new board members to be skilled system thinkers. On the other hand, ideally some board members should be radically open-minded (see Ray Dalio's suggestion quoted above) with curiosity and imagination for what they do not know that could be important for the firm's long-term performance. In addition, they would have a nose for what specific new knowledge, once obtained, may significantly improve performance. Institutional shareholders should make changes in the selection process for new board members a top priority.

Contrast the above with conventional board-member criteria such as leadership experience (preferably in larger firms), knowledge of the firm's businesses, and diversity. Interestingly, a board is viewed as becoming more diverse by bringing in new board members who are nonwhite or nonmale but usually have made their successful careers by attaining high leadership positions in command-and-control organizations. However, the problem is that this leaves undisturbed a shared worldview at the board level that sees the firm in terms of hierarchical control.

Let's consider an example of how these radically open-minded, curious board members could see problems and opportunities not otherwise on the radar screen for boards. Many large firms have hierarchical, multidivisional command-and-control organizational structures that originated with General Motors in the 1920s (Johnson 1978). Management's objective is to forecast, plan, and control using accounting budget targets. The divisional businesses have a hierarchy in which accounting targets are tailored and passed down to lower levels in the hierarchy. Such an organizational structure is best suited to a stable environment; even then it can stymie the nurturing and sustaining of a knowledge-building culture in which employees at all levels are treated as value creators. Today, the CEOs of many large firms moved up the corporate ladder by excelling in this command-and-control environment, and this experience has shaped their worldviews. A radical idea for boards is to transition these large (and often bureaucratic) pyramid organizations to much flatter organizations in order to improve innovation and long-term performance.

Much has been written about flat organizations that drive decision-making to lower levels in the organization. Two large firms leading the trend to flatter organizations are the Haier Group and Nucor (Hamel and Zanini 2020). The Haier Group is a large Chinese multinational leader in home appliances and consumer electronics. Zhang Rumin was CEO for three decades and led the firm's evolution to its current structure that has eliminated the conventional multiple layers of a hierarchical system, replaced by thousands of microenterprises that strive for zero distance between employees and customers plus win-win relationships in partnering with other firms.

Nucor is the largest steel producer and recycler of scrap (input to their steel operations) in the United States. Ken Iverson became CEO in 1965 and for the next three decades guided the firm's adoption of leading-edge technology; and importantly, he shaped Nucor's culture consistent with a flat organization. Iverson provides insights as to decentralization, including flatter organizational structures:

> If your success depends heavily on uniformity and consistency, centralized decision making may be justified. If your success relies more on innovation and flexibility, you should make a conscious effort to push decision-making power down. . . .

> I'm not so much a champion of decentralization as I am an advocate for decisiveness. Managers at all levels need to assess what is most crucial for the operations they manage and—based on that assessment—choose where the locus of decision-making power should reside. Then they must implement that choice thoroughly, and stick to their choice over the long term. (Iverson and Varian 1998, 42–44)

Systems thinking suggests a multitude of cause-and-effect relationships involved with changing a command-and-control organization. An important consideration is the budget process at the heart of control (Joseph and Gaba 2020). Jensen (2003, 379) summarizes the lived experience of people who negotiate budget targets with their boss: "Eliminating budget/target-induced gaming from the management system will eliminate one of the major forces leading to the general loss of integrity in organizations. People are taught to lie in these pervasive budgeting systems because if they tell the truth they often get punished and if they lie they get rewarded."

What might happen if a large firm managed with conventional budget targets actually eliminated budgets? How's that for radical open-mindedness? Bill Anderson did just that as CEO of Genentech in 2017 and later repeated this shock treatment as CEO of Roche Pharmaceuticals. Here is Anderson's reasoning:

> There's this system where you have to have an arbitrary budget fixed months in advance. When you're building a budget in January, who knows what you're going to need in November? And the hierarchical approval process destroyed accountability and initiative. We got rid of targets and we got rid of budgets. . . . Since we stopped budgeting [at Roche], spending is down, and performance is up. . . . We couldn't simply make

> incremental changes to a broken system. We had to go deep and look at things like the *purpose* of a large organization, *question assumptions* about the role of management. . . . We're telling people to stop doing things that don't directly serve patients today or lead to a new medicine for tomorrow. . . . I could remove budgets and know that people would do the right things, because the underlying fabric—people and purpose—was solid. Without the right circumstances, another leader in another company might not be able to. (2020; italics added)

Keep in mind that the Pragmatic Theory of the Firm emphasizes how understanding connections in a complex system, such as the firm, enables awareness of what one does not know. For example, do board members have a defensible answer to the question: Is their approved CEO compensation viewed as fair in the eyes of employees? For board members to say that they use compensation consultants is not a defensible answer. However, let's consider hypothetical board members who are radically open-minded, humble about what they do not know, and curious. What questions might they ask? Perhaps: Do more layers of control lead to higher CEO compensation? Would a much flatter organization improve a firm's culture and its performance? Would a flatter organization bring CEOs much closer to employees doing the work and lead to lower CEO compensation in the spirit of fairness and sustaining a desirable culture? These are the kinds of better questions (awareness of connections) that can lead to new useful knowledge.

There is a need for academic research that sheds light on context (as noted by Iverson and Anderson), radical change in organizational structure, and firm performance. Imagine the progress that could be achieved if researchers partnered with boards of directors willing to experiment with significant changes in their firms. A beginning point is for institutional shareholders to realize the advantages of a board of directors that is diverse in terms of their worldviews, that is, new directors who have had leadership roles involved with innovation and preferably in organizations other than large command-and-control hierarchies.

Conclusions

Capitalism facilitates knowledge building, competition, and efficient allocation of resources, thereby sustaining large-scale value creation. Capitalism is powered by imagination and change, leading to a rising standard of living. Moreover, the seemingly never-ending debates about shareholder capitalism versus stakeholder capitalism can be defused by understanding that maximizing shareholder value is best positioned not as the purpose of the firm but as the result of a firm successfully achieving its four-part purpose.

Knowledge building is the result of effective traversing of the Knowledge Building Loop guided by imagination that is focused on understanding a complex situation, or solving a problem, or achieving an innovation that improves customer experience (value creation). Imagination is gaining momentum in the business world as a source of innovation and not merely being relegated to artists and writers (Reeves and Fuller 2021). In his 2018 Amazon shareholders letter, the CEO Jeff Bezos (2019) discusses imagination:

> The biggest needle movers will be things that customers don't know to ask for. We must invent on their behalf. We have to tap into our own inner imagination about what's possible.
>
> AWS [Amazon Web Services] itself—as a whole—is an example. No one asked for AWS. No one. Turns out the world was in fact ready and hungry for an offering like AWS but didn't know it. We had a hunch, followed our curiosity, took

the necessary financial risks, and began building—reworking, experimenting, and iterating countless times as we proceeded.

Reworking, experimenting, and iterating—that is the Knowledge Building Loop. The rationale for a corporate governance upgrade has its roots in this loop and the Pragmatic Theory of the Firm. Note that the *worldviews*, shared by board members whose career successes were achieved in large command-and-control firms, shape how they *perceive* the world. A rethinking of the selection process for new board members is warranted. Institutional shareholders with worldviews rooted in the long term could orchestrate a new selection process to the ultimate benefit of all stakeholders in our capitalistic society.

NOTES

[1] Bartley J. Madden. 2023. "Understanding the Benefits of Capitalism through the Lens of a New Theory of the Firm." *Capitalism and Society*. 17(1) article 2.

[2] Bartley J. Madden. 2012. "Management's Worldview: Four Critical Points about Reality, Language, and Knowledge Building to Improve Organizational Performance." *Journal of Organizational Computing and Electronic Commerce* 22(4): 334-346.

References

Anderson, William N. 2020. "CEO Of Roche Pharmaceuticals on Serving Patients During the Pandemic and Driving Transformational Change." Interview by David Benjamin and David Komlos. *Forbes*, June 29, 2020. https://www.forbes.com/sites/benjaminkomlos/2020/06/29/ceo-of-roche-pharmaceuticals -on-serving-patients-during-the-pandemic-and-driving-transformational-change/?sh=446c1d 993527.

Barrett, Lisa Feldman. 2020. *Seven and a Half Lessons about the Brain*. Boston: Houghton Mifflin Harcourt.

Bereiter, Carl. 2009. "Innovation in the Absence of Principled Knowledge: The Case of the Wright Brothers." *Creativity and Innovation Management* 18 (3): 234–41. https://doi.org/10.1111/j.1467-8691.2009.00528.x.

Bezos, Jeff. 2019. "2018 Letter to Shareholders." *Amazon News*, April 11, 2019. https://www.aboutamazon.com/news/company-news/2018-letter-to-shareholders.

Cerasoli, Christopher P., Jessica M. Nicklin, and M. T. Ford. 2014. "Intrinsic Motivation and Extrinsic Incentives Jointly Predict Performance: A 40-Year Meta-Analysis." *Psychological Bulletin* (140) 4: 980–1008. https://doi.org/10.1037/a0035661.

Chalmers, Dominic. 2022. "Collectivist Perspectives on Crony Capitalism." *Academy of Management Perspectives* 36 (4): 1049–57. https://doi.org/10.5465/amp.2021.0195.

Dalio, Ray. 2017. *Principles*. New York: Simon & Schuster.

Felin, Teppo, Alfonso Gambardella, Scott Stern, and Todd Zenger. 2019. "Lean Startup and the Business Model: Experimentation Revisited." *Long Range Planning* 53 (4): article 101889. https://doi.org/10.1016/j.lrp.2019.06.002.

Felin, Teppo, Jan Koenderink, and Joachim I. Krueger. 2017. "Rationality, Perception, and the All-Seeing Eye." *Psychonomic Bulletin & Review* 24 (4): 1040–59. https://doi.org/10.3758/s13423-016-1198-z.

Frigo, Mark L., and Bartley J. Madden. 2020. "Strategic Life-Cycle Analysis: The Role of the CFO." *Strategic Finance*, October 1, 2020, 33–39. https://sfmagazine.com/articles/2020/october/strategic-life-cycle-analysis-the-role-of-the-cfo.

Garicano, Luis, and Yanhui Wu. 2012. "Knowledge, Communication, and Organizational Capabilities." *Organization Science* 23 (5): 1382–97. https://doi.org/10.1287/orsc.1110.0723.

Garud, Raghu, Philipp Tuertscher, and Andrew H. Van de Ven. 2013. "Perspectives on Innovation Processes." *Academy of Management Annals* 7 (1): 773–817. https://doi.org/10.5465/19416520.2013.791066.

Hamel, Gary, and Michele Zanini. 2020. *Humanocracy: Creating Organizations as Amazing as the People Inside Them.* Boston: Harvard Business Review Press.

Henderson, Rebecca. 2021. "Innovation in the 21st Century: Architectural Change, Purpose, and the Challenges of Our Time." *Management Science* 67 (9): 5479–88. https://doi.org/10.1287/mnsc.2020.3746.

Holland, David A., and Bryant A. Matthews. 2018. *Beyond Earnings: Applying the HOLT CFROI and Economic Profit Framework.* Hoboken, NJ: John Wiley & Sons.

Iverson, Ken, and Tom Varian. 1998. *Plain Talk: Lessons from a Business Maverick.* Hoboken, NJ: John Wiley & Sons.

Jackson, Michael C. 2019. *Critical Systems Thinking and the Management of Complexity.* Hoboken, NJ: John Wiley & Sons.

Jakab, Peter L. 1990. *Visions of a Flying Machine: The Wright Brothers and the Process of Invention.* Washington, DC: Smithsonian Institution Press.

Jensen, Michael C. 2003. "Paying People to Lie: The Truth about the Budgeting Process." *European Financial Management* 9 (3): 379–406. https://doi.org/10.1111/1468-036X.00226.

Johnson, H. Thomas. 1978. "Management Accounting in an Early Multidivisional Organization: General Motors in the 1920s." *Business History Review* 52 (4): 490–517. https://doi.org/10.2307/3113416.

Joseph, John, and Vibha Gaba. 2020. "Organizational Structure, Information Processing, and Decision-Making: A Retrospective and Road Map for Research." *Academy of Management Annals* 14 (1): 267–302. https://doi.org/10.5465/annals.2017.0103.

Kerr, William R., Ramana Nanda, and Matthew Rhodes-Kropf. 2014. "Entrepreneurship as Experimentation." *Journal of Economic Perspectives* 28 (3): 25-48. https://doi.org/10.1257/jep.28.3.25.

Klein, Peter G., R. Michael Holmes Jr., Nicolai Foss, Siri Terjesen, and Justin Pepe. 2022. "Capitalism, Cronyism, and Management Scholarship: A Call for Clarity." *Academy of Management Perspectives* 36 (1): 6–29. https://doi.org/10.5465/amp.2019.0198.

Lotto, Beau R. 2017. *Deviate: The Science of Seeing Differently.* New York: Hachette Books.

Madden, Bartley J. 2020. *Value Creation Principles: The Pragmatic Theory of the Firm Begins with Purpose and Ends with Sustainable Capitalism.* Hoboken, NJ: John Wiley & Sons.

Madden, Bartley J. 2021. "The Pragmatic Theory of the Firm." *Journal of Applied Corporate Finance* 33 (1): 98–110. https://doi.org/10.1111/jacf.12448.

Madden, Bartley J. 2023. "Bet on Innovation, Not Environmental, Social, and Governance Metrics, to Lead the Net Zero Transition." *Systems Research and Behavioral Science* 40 (3): 417–28. https://doi.org/10.1002/sres.2915.

Marken, Richard S. and Brittany Horth. 2011. "When Causality Does Not Imply Correlation: More Spadework at the Foundation of Scientific Psychology." *Psychological Reports* 108 (3): 943–54. https://doi.org/10.2466/03.PR0.108.3.943-954.

Martin, Roger L. 2002. *A New Way to Think: Your Guide to Superior Management Effectiveness.* Boston: Harvard Business Review Press.

McCullough, David G. 2015. *The Wright Brothers.* New York: Simon & Schuster.

Mazzucato, Mariana. 2021. *Mission Economy: A Moonshot Guide to Changing Capitalism.* New York: Harper Business.

Montgomery, John B., and Mark Van Clieaf. 2023. *Net Zero Business Models: Winning in the Global Net Zero Economy.* Hoboken, NJ: John Wiley & Sons.

Ohno, Taiichi. (1978) 1988. *Toyota Production System: Beyond Large-Scale Production.* New York: Productivity Press.

Packard, Mark D. 2022. *Entrepreneurial Valuation: An Entrepreneur's Guide to Getting into the Minds of Customers.* Berlin: Walter de Gruyter.

Pendleton-Jullian, Ann M., and John Seely Brown. 2018. *Design Unbound: Designing for Emergence in a White Water World.* 2 vols. Cambridge, MA: MIT Press.

Polman, Paul. 2014. "Tackle Sustainability Challenges with a Systems-Based Approach." *International Business Times*, January 20, 2014. https://www.ibtimes.co.uk/unilever-ceo-paul-polman-tackle-sustainability-challenges-systems-based-approach-1433024.

Powers, William T. 1973. "Feedback: Beyond Behaviorism." *Science* 179 (4071): 351–56. https://doi.org/10.1126/science.179.4071.351.

Rangan, Subramanian. 2018. *Capitalism beyond Mutuality? Perspectives Integrating Philosophy and Social Science.* Oxford: Oxford University Press.

Reeves, Martin, and Jack Fuller. 2021. *The Imagination Machine: How to Spark New Ideas and Create Your Company's Future.* Boston: Harvard Business Review Press.

Rhodes, Richard. 2018. *Energy: A Human History.* New York: Simon & Schuster.

Shapiro, Stephen M. 2020. *Invisible Solutions: 25 Lenses That Reframe and Help Solve*

Difficult Business Problems. Herndon, VA: Amplify Publishing.

Smith, Brad. 2016. "Intuit CEO: The Most Important Job of a CEO." *Observer*. January 28, 2016. https://observer.com/2016/01/intuit-ceo-the-most-important-job-of-a-ceo.

Weick, Karl E. 1989. "Theory Construction as Disciplined Imagination." *Academy of Management Review* 14 (4): 516–31. https://doi.org/10.5465/amr.1989.4308376.

Wright, Wilbur, and Orville Wright. (1951) 1996. *Miracle at Kitty Hawk*. Edited by Fred C. Kelly. New York: Da Capo Press.

Wright, Wilbur, and Orville Wright. 2001. *The Papers of Wilbur and Orville Wright: Including the Chanute-Wright Papers*. 2 vols. Edited by Marvin W. McFarland. New York: McGraw-Hill.

CHAPTER 4

Journal of Applied Corporate Finance[1]

THE PRAGMATIC THEORY OF THE FIRM

Bartley J. Madden

In 1992, Alfred Chandler wrote:

> I am convinced that the unit of analysis must be the firm, rather than transactions or contractual relations entered into by the firm. Only by focusing on the firm can microeconomics theory explain why this legal, contracting, transacting entity has been the instrument in capitalist economics for carrying out the processes of production and distribution, for increasing productivity, and for propelling economic growth and transformation.[2]

It is difficult to disagree with Chandler. The firm is the crux of a capitalist economy. Take away the firm and you take away growth, investment, value creation, and dynamism. Yet, neoclassical economics has continued to neglect the firm's main activity—running a business.[3] Various theories of the firm have emerged that either emphasize what the developers consider particularly important to a firm's long-term performance or focus on organizational issues, such as the assignment of decision rights and design of incentives, and the optimal integration of the value chain.[4]

The pragmatic theory of the firm

The pragmatic theory begins with a statement of the firm's purpose and treats the firm as a holistic system. The theory accordingly views all components as interrelated, rather than analyzing each component separately and in isolation, as has been customary. The theory then focuses on the firm's knowledge-building proficiency as the primary intangible asset for achieving the firm's purpose. The life-cycle, financial-performance framework is used to illustrate the practical benefits of the pragmatic theory, especially improved decision-making by management. The pragmatic theory is expected to encourage new and more fruitful research programs on the workings of the firm, while solidifying the firm as the fundamental unit of analysis for economic progress.[5]

The key components of the firm, as can be seen in Figure 1, are knowledge-building proficiency, work, innovation, resource allocation, and firm risk. The system's financial results are evaluated in the context of the life-cycle framework, including competitive fade and shareholder returns. We could have drawn Figure 1 with spaghetti-like lines connecting each of the boxes. Though visually less attractive, this picture would more accurately reflect the complex, networked nature of the business firm. The pragmatic theory of the firm fosters insights by avoiding oversimplifications and establishing new holistic connections.

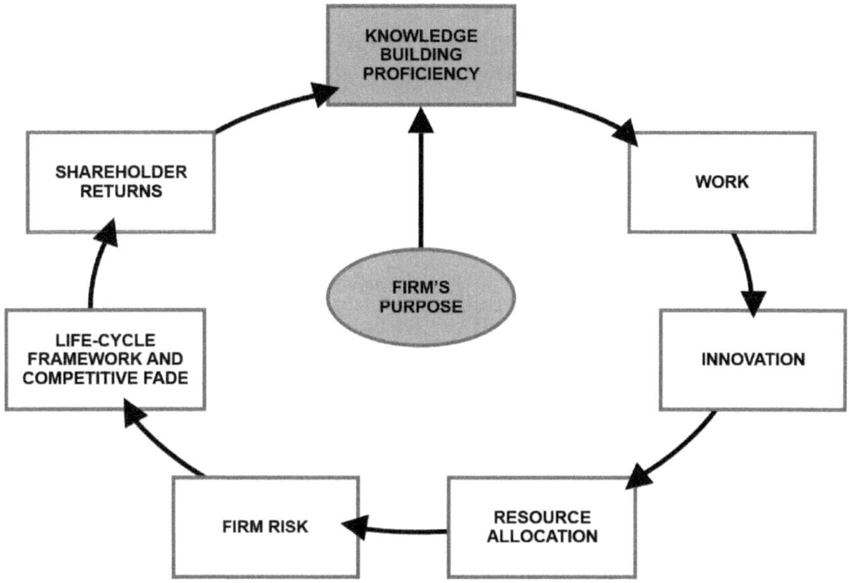

Components of the Pragmatic Theory of the Firm
Source: Madden 2020, 31

Gaining clarity about the firm's purpose is of utmost importance not only for managing the firm but also for positioning the firm as the primary means, at least in capitalist societies, to innovate and achieve progress that lifts all boats. Furthermore, I argue that a firm's knowledge-building proficiency relative to its competitors is the primary determinant of a firm's long-term performance.

Capabilities that benefit a firm today may be much less valuable in the future. How often do we hear that capability X is the key to a firm's competitive advantage? Nevertheless, the focus should be on improving capability X over time. Such continuous improvement then circles back to a firm's knowledge-building proficiency, which requires people at all levels of the firm to have a commitment to, and even passion for, dealing with uncertainty, solving problems, and participating in the development and commercialization of breakthrough innovations.

In the remainder of this article, I will explain how and why the pragmatic theory is more useful than other theories of the firm.[6]

The firm's purpose

The purpose of the firm can be decomposed into four mutually reinforcing goals:[7]

- *Communicating a vision* that can inspire and motivate employees to work for a firm that is committed to behaving ethically and making the world a better place.
- *Surviving and Prospering* through continual gains in efficiency and sustained innovation, which depend on a firm's knowledge-building proficiency. Importantly, nothing works long term if the firm fails to earn at least the cost of capital.
- Working continuously to sustain *win-win relationships* with all the firm's stakeholders.
- *Taking care of future generations.* Management needs a genuine commitment to the sustainability of the environment, with particular attention to the design of products and manufacturing processes to minimize waste and pollution, which again depends on the firm's knowledge-building proficiency.

The four-part purpose addresses the needs of all stakeholders. It answers the question of why employees should be genuinely enthusiastic about their jobs. It makes palpable the need for a cost-of-capital guidepost so that the firm can survive and prosper. In so doing, it provides a logical and comprehensive framework for dealing with complex issues such as expenditure decisions for R&D and manufacturing capacity, and decisions about new employee benefits and local community programs so that both the firm and society can get the most out of limited resources.

Knowledge building

As previously noted, the pragmatic theory identifies the firm's knowledge-building proficiency as the primary determinant of the firm's long-term performance. To be sure, most researchers who support a knowledge-based view focus on groups, business units, or the entire firm. My preference is to focus on the individual. Robert Grant, an early proponent of the knowledge-based view, argued: "The emphasis upon the role of the individual as the primary actor in knowledge creation and the principal repository of knowledge, I believe, is essential to piercing the veil of organizational knowledge and clarifying the role of organizations in the creation and application of knowledge."[8]

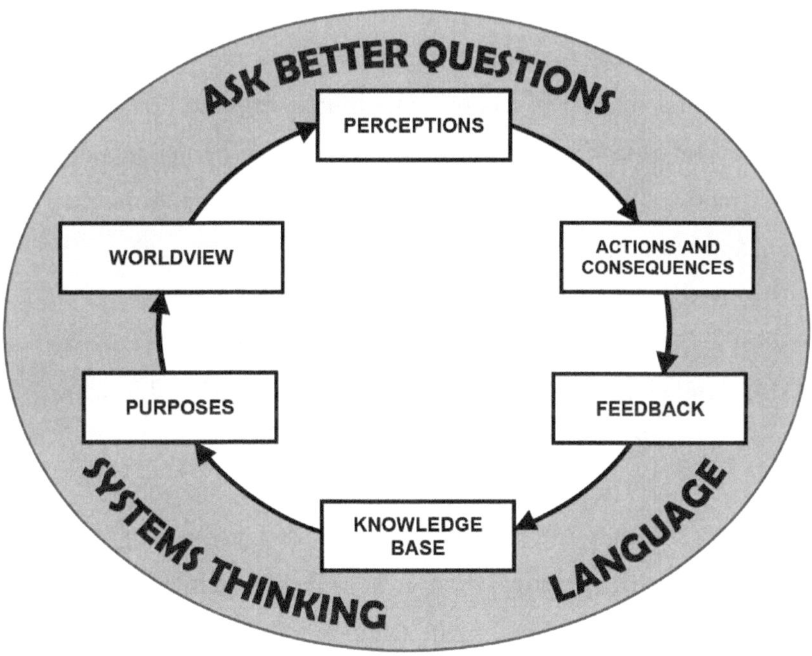

Figure 2. The Knowledge-Building Loop.
Source: *Value Creation Principles: The Pragmatic Theory of the Firm Begins with Purpose and Ends with Sustainable Capitalism*, by Bartley J. Madden.

When knowledge building becomes an integral part of every employee's job, both job satisfaction and retention of key employees improves.[9] Such a culture unleashes creativity and motivates employees to solve problems and create new opportunities by discovering obsolete assumptions and unraveling root causes. A knowledge-building loop like the one illustrated in Figure 2 emphasizes the components required to build knowledge, and especially, the critical role of one's worldview, assumptions, and language.[10] Attention to how we build knowledge offers insights into improving business performance, including the performance of top management and the board of directors. Rita McGrath writes as follows about a lack of imagination that leads to unquestioned acceptance of key business assumptions:

> Business inflection points undermine the very assumptions on which a business is based and which have come to be taken as "facts" by most decision-makers. It is often difficult for leaders to imagine a different world. It is this failure of imagination that so often leads to strategic surprise . . . It is crucial . . . that data that challenge embedded orthodoxies be presented along with information that supports the common view. Otherwise . . . people will continue to do business in the echo chamber of their existing assumptions.[11]

We go through life traversing a knowledge-building loop while continuously learning which actions help best to achieve our purposes. The components of Figure 2 serve as guideposts that help audit how we know what we think we know. The knowledge base contains assumptions of varying degrees of reliability. One's worldview represents ideas and beliefs through which we interpret and interact with the world. A worldview that favors a deeper understanding of causality and nonlinear system complexities improves one's knowledge base, leading to more efficacious actions that produce desired consequences. Brain scientists affirm that our perceptions are based on memories that facilitate predictions via analogy to the past.[12] We see what our brains tell us to see.[13] Especially important is orchestrating feedback that can overcome our automatic reliance on the past and reveal obsolete assumptions earlier than otherwise.

The preeminent role of language shown in Figure 2 can be attributed to its pervasive influence throughout the knowledge-building process. Language itself plays a major role in camouflaging assumptions while greatly simplifying the world.[14] One key insight from the knowledge-building loop is the importance of continuous awareness of the need for constructive skepticism about strongly held assumptions that influence our perceptions and our actions. Scrutiny of the language we use can help discover the root cause of problems and lead to asking better questions.

A classic example involves the goal of *minimize accounting costs* for operation A that feeds material to B along a manufacturing line. The hidden assumption in the italicized words is that A is independent of B. However, if B is the bottleneck (key constraint) in the manufacturing line, then the installation of a faster machine at A will reduce A's accounting costs but worsen B's situation and degrade the overall system performance. Systems thinking can overcome a misplaced emphasis on local optimization typically caused by linear cause-and-effect thinking.[15]

Keep in mind that behavior within the firm is influenced by performance measurements based on our Old Economy accounting system rooted in tangible assets. Management attention to improving the performance of intangible assets should accelerate as our language improves for talking about, and measuring, intangibles including knowledge-building skills. This is not an abstract point. Improved problem-solving entails fast and effective traversing of the knowledge-building loop.

A key component of this loop is perceptions. Consider how frequently a business problem is discussed and a solution devised based solely on perceptions derived from accounting data in a written report. Quite the opposite way of perceiving situations has been adopted by Lean practitioners who have studied the Toyota Production System. They frequently use the Japanese term *gemba,* which is the place where value is created. A gemba walk is about observing a process for yourself in order to provide new perceptions and feedback about the reliability of one's assumptions (knowledge base).[16] Better management of human capital (intangible assets) should follow advancements in language. We are in the early stage of the development of a language for intangibles.

Today's cost accounting language promotes local efficiencies and interferes with value stream analyses that focus on all the processes to deliver a final product or service to the customer. Value stream analyses run horizontally, cutting across the firm's many functional silos. We need a new accounting language to evolve that is attuned to optimizing the overall system (firm); facilitates value stream analyses; and treats human capital in general, and knowledge-building proficiency in particular, as performance-driving assets.[17]

Consider how language silently guides thinking in conventional market research with categories based on customer demographics and comparison of product features with competing products. Now consider the shift in thinking facilitated by different language in Clayton Christensen's theory of jobs to be done.[18] The core idea is to understand the *job* that customers *hire* the product to do. This way of thinking explains why the popular QuickBooks accounting software, developed by Intuit, dominates the competition even though it offers only a fraction of the features offered by competing software packages and sells at a substantial premium. QuickBooks excels at helping customers easily complete the job they want done, especially avoiding accounting technicalities.

Note the importance of the knowledge-building process to Intuit, the accounting software firm that developed QuickBooks. Intuit has a $90 billion market value and a stellar long-term performance track record. Former CEO Brad Smith points out:

> Job one in creating a culture is building a purpose-driven culture . . . At Intuit, our mission is to improve our customers' financial lives so profoundly they can't imagine going back to the old way . . . One way leaders can create an action-oriented environment is to match inspiration with rigor, adopting a rapid-experimentation culture. Great ideas are simply hypotheses unless matched with tangible proof they deliver meaningful impact. A rapid experimentation culture cuts through hierarchy (especially if leaders hold their own ideas to the same scrutiny of testing), creating an environment where everyone can innovate, and "debate" turns into "doing."[19]

A purpose-driven and rapid-experimentation culture neatly ties into the pragmatic theory. A knowledge-building culture is the "behind-the-scenes" driver of a firm's long-term financial performance, win-win relationships, and taking care of future generations.

One major takeaway from the pragmatic theory is the importance of management's assigning high priority to improving knowledge-building proficiency, on a par with the attention given to improving conventional accounting-based metrics. Management can focus on a process for continual improvement, but still go after immediate big payoffs:

> Commission a core-belief identification squad . . . calling on a diverse, cross-functional working group to go hunting for the firm's most deeply-held assumptions about itself and the industry in which it operates. The best-functioning squads include a significant share of younger, newer employees, who

are less likely to be invested in current orthodoxies. Their efforts are most fruitful when the team is prepared to raise thorny issues and challenge entrenched beliefs, using methods ranging from reality checks—What industry are we in? Who are our customers?—to more provocative explorations: What 10 things would you never hear customers say about our business?[20]

Firm risk

Firm risk is created and amplified by obstacles to achieving the firm's purpose. Firm risk involves not only controls to avoid bad (value destruction) experiences, but also a way of working that generates opportunities for good (value creation) experiences. Consequently, management and the board need to nurture and sustain a culture that embraces experimentation and the freedom to question key assumptions at all levels of the firm.

Knowledge building and managing firm risk are opposite sides of the same coin. Project risk is typically associated with uncertainty, difficulty in formulating plans and control processes, and potential wide variation in operating results. Knowledge building is similarly associated with the same characteristics leading to experimentation, feedback, and testing the validity of key assumptions. *Build knowledge to better manage firm risk and create long-term value.*

Firm risk offers a complementary view to what is taught in business schools about investor risk. The latter is based on CAPM and the covariance of a firm's stock price with the general market captured as Beta. Firm risk increases (decreases) in lockstep with changes that degrade (improve) the likelihood of achieving the firm's purpose. This perspective comports with David Koenig's approach to corporate governance: "Businesses exist to take risk . . . We know that if risk is always seen negatively, we will be making sub-optimal decisions about taking it . . .

the fear of taking risks is the surest way to realize failure, as our customers will ultimately leave us for better alternatives, or through simply finding little new value in what we do."[21]

An increase in firm risk, all else equal, means a greater likelihood for negative surprises as to future financial results. Investors eventually perceive an increase in firm risk and, all else equal, the firm's stock price declines to a level that adequately compensates investors for the increased likelihood of future shortfalls in the firm's financial performance. Striking examples of increased firm risk are the unethical behavior of Enron's top management and Union Carbide's disregard for maintenance and safety leading to more than 10,000 deaths from the explosion at its chemical plant in Bhopal, India in 1984. Firm risk is long-term oriented, rooted in the firm's foundational purpose, and engages broadly with all of the firm's stakeholders. There can be a substantial time lag between a change in firm risk and investor perception. In each of the six years leading up to its bankruptcy at the end of 2001, Enron was named "America's Most Innovative Company" by *Fortune.*

A holistic view of the firm facilitates managing firm risk. In contrast, isolating on just one activity such as innovation with a singular focus on financial gain can easily become counter-productive to value creation. Prior to the 2007-2009 financial crisis, many banks developed "innovative" products that boosted near-term earnings, such as negative amortization loans in which the early monthly payments were less than the interest expense all the while increasing the principal owed. These loans encouraged buyers to speculate on steadily rising homes prices. We know how that worked out.

A holistic view connects these "innovative" loans to the firm's purpose, specifically win-win partnerships (most importantly with customers). Such a holistic view was embraced by management and the board of BB&T, the best-performing large bank during the financial crisis. The CEO and board chairman John Allison noted that BB&T chose not to offer negative amortization loans for ethical reasons. His explanation of BB&T's culture resonates with the pragmatic theory's four-part purpose of the firm:

> If you want to have passion and energy in your life, you must have a sense of purpose in your work . . . I ask the employees of BB&T: Are you truly making the world a better place to live through your work? Are you really helping your clients achieve economic success and financial security? Are you providing the quality of advice that ensures that they make better decisions? You should never do anything that you believe will not be in your client's best interest, even if you can make a profit in the short term. . . . Life is about creating win-win relationships.[22]

What is the primary, quantifiable long-term measure of a company's success or failure in managing its firm risk? I identify it as *competitive fade*, which will now be explained as part of the life-cycle framework.

The life-cycle framework and competitive fade

Figure 3 illustrates transitional stages in a firm's life cycle that capture the dynamics of its profitability and growth in a competitive environment. In the *high-innovation* stage, the key assumptions of the business model need to be validated and the sooner the better. Successful commercialization leads to economic returns well above the cost of capital along with significant asset growth. At the *competitive fade* stage, competitors attempt to duplicate and improve upon the originator's innovation. The subsequent fade rates depend on competitive advantage. A more descriptive label, however, that reflects the process involved is effectiveness in managing firm risk. This drills into the mindset of top management and the board for blending how the firm develops value-creation projects and, on occasion (hopefully), breakthrough innovations (upside gains), while still maintaining control of business processes (downside losses) in line with the firm's four-part purpose.

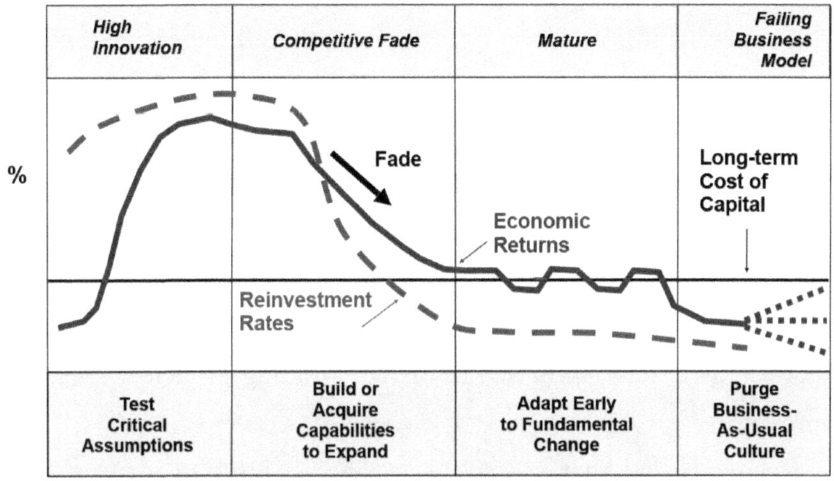

Figure 3. The Life-Cycle Framework
Source: *Value Creation Principles: The Pragmatic Theory of the Firm Begins with Purpose and Ends with Sustainable Capitalism*, by Bartley J. Madden.

Over the long term, the firm's economic returns fade toward the cost of capital and its asset growth rates regress toward a growth rate close to the economy's growth rate. At the *mature* stage where cost-of-capital (average) economic returns are earned, managing firm risk should definitely take center stage. New investments with the promise of earning value-creating returns above the cost of capital can depress profitability in the near term while taking resources away from existing businesses that are paying the bills. Consequently, overinvestment can easily occur in businesses that offer the perceived comfort of being in control but offer little hope for future economic returns above the cost of capital.[23] And when the managements and boards of mature firms prove consistently ineffective in managing firm risk, their firm's economic returns fade significantly below the cost of capital. This *failing business model stage* requires purging of a business-as-usual culture and complacency and, most often, down-sizing as part of a restructuring to improve how value is delivered to customers.

To prevent this outcome, management should undertake a number of critical steps shown at the bottom of Figure 3 that are appropriate for each stage of the firm's life-cycle. In terms of managing firm risk, these tasks are especially important both in avoiding the downside (unfavorable fade) and preparing to take advantage of the upside (favorable fade), which reflects the two sides of firm risk.

The long-term fade of a firm's economic returns can typically be explained as a function of its knowledge-building proficiency versus its competitors'.

Keep in mind that successful knowledge building depends upon a keen awareness of context, i.e., the firm's unique internal makeup (intangible human assets and tangible assets) and the changing external environment. Take the case of the biopharma company Illumina, which demonstrated a high level of proficiency in knowledge building (managing firm risk for the upside) as it became the leader in large-scale analysis of genetic variation and function. Illumina did not begin as a startup with best-in-class technology. Rather, Jay Flatley, CEO from 1999 to 2016, was especially skilled in monitoring competitors (see Figure 2) to identify where Illumina's technology was lagging. Flatley responded to these "gaps" through a series of acquisitions, including the critically important acquisition of Solexa in 2007.

How did Flatley orchestrate the scaling up of Illumina to dominate its industry?

> One of the really important things we did, early on, was structure our product development process in a way where we could very efficiently run a large number of projects simultaneously. This is

> what has given us the ability to scale, in size and complexity and number of projects, and still be able to manage with a limited number of top executives. That's because of how we empower our teams to go off and do great things. They only have to come back to us under a very fixed set of circumstances. We [in management] can set the strategy and direction and talk about specifications. They can do the execution, which they are really good at.[24]

Life-cycle track records: The case of John Deere

In 1837, John Deere, a blacksmith, developed an innovative plow for farmers, which led to the firm that bears his name and today provides leading products and services in agriculture, turf, construction, and forestry. Figure 4 displays Deere's 1960-2018 life-cycle track record. In the top panel, Deere's economic returns are calculated as CFROIs, which are adjusted for inflation and other biases (e.g., R&D outlays are capitalized) present in as-reported accounting statements.[25] Inflation adjustments are required in order to more accurately measure levels and trends over long time periods. The benchmark, inflation-adjusted cost of capital of 6% is shown as a horizontal line.[26]

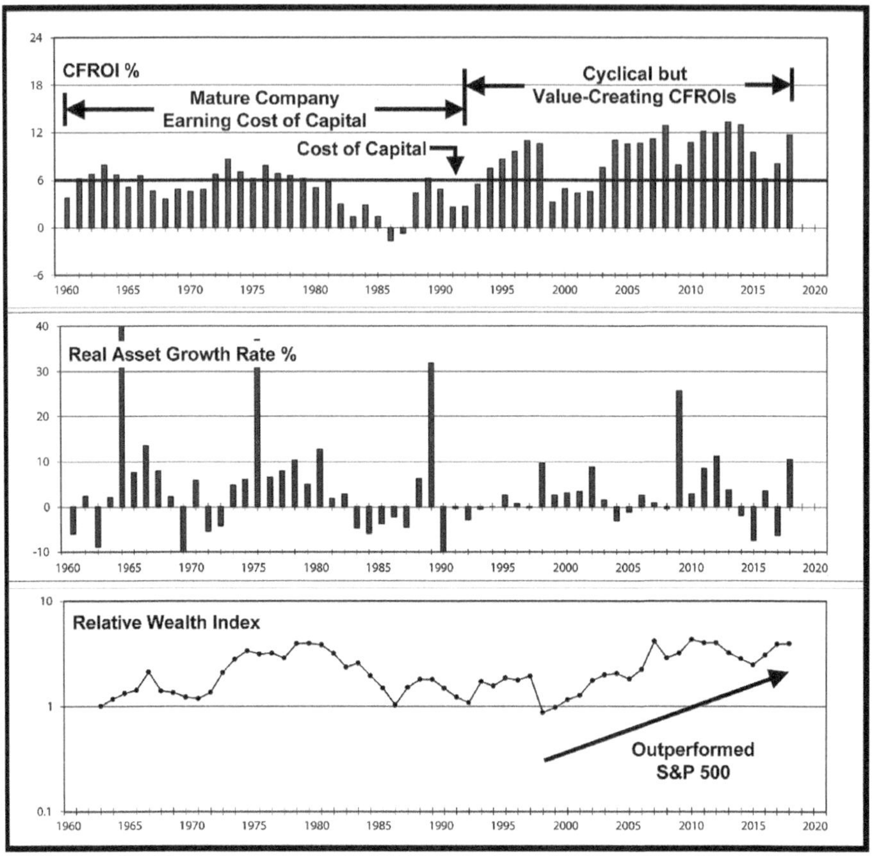

Figure 4. Deere & Company 1960-2018
Source: Based on data from Credit Suisse HOLT global database.

The top panel of Figure 4 indicates that, from 1960 to the early 2000s, Deere was in the mature life-cycle stage with CFROIs approximating the cost of capital. Over the next two decades, Deere transitioned to earning cyclical but mostly value-creating CFROIs exceeding the cost of capital. The middle panel displays Deere's modest real (inflation-adjusted) asset growth rates over time with occasional spikes due to substantial acquisitions. The bottom panel displays a relative wealth index, i.e., a stock's total return relative to the S&P 500 total return. A rising trend in the relative wealth index is attributable to outperformance; a flat trend reflects market-matching shareholder returns, and a declining trend underperformance of the S&P 500 index. Since 2000, Deere has generated a mostly rising relative wealth index. This outperformance of Deere's stock reflected investors' recognition of a new higher level of CFROIs that exceeded earlier expectations for a continuation of an "Old Economy" mature firm.

From the perspective of firm risk, management successfully evolved from a product-centric business to embrace the digital world with a platform-centric capability. Customers today benefit from Deere's precision agriculture services that use sensors on their machines and probes in the soil plus data collection and software that increases yield and decreases costs. Such evolution was the result of management's ability to shift the focus of its resource allocation from business-as-usual expansion of Old Economy products to early adaptation to the information-based New Economy.

Let's take a deeper look at Deere's transition with reference to the pragmatic theory of the firm illustrated previously. In the early 2000s, Deere was like many mature firms providing operating returns at, or slightly less than, the cost of capital with a culture, or accepted way of doing things, that was deeply engrained in how employees worked. We should not underestimate the high degree of difficulty for management of a large mature firm like Deere to transition to a value-creating firm and sustain economic returns in excess of the cost of capital.[27]

Referring back to Figure 1, we can take any component such as work or innovation and tell a story about how implementation of lean manufacturing or a heightened focus on strategic R&D contributed to Deere's improved performance. However, there is a particularly important story about Deere's performance and the link to job creation, economic growth, win-win relationships, and taking care of future generations. Telling that story is best facilitated by the pragmatic theory of the firm.

In analyzing any complex system, such as a firm, it makes sense to begin with the purpose of the system and pinpoint what, if any, are the shortfalls in achieving the purpose. Let's focus on "survive and prosper," which is one part of the pragmatic theory's four-part purpose of the firm. Along these lines, it was earlier noted that nothing works long term if the firm fails to earn at least the cost of capital. Of utmost importance is for management and the board to assert that cost-of-capital performance is unacceptable. Acceptance today of earning only the cost of capital is a recipe for earning far less than the cost of capital tomorrow as more performance-oriented competitors increasingly better serve customers.

Basic finance tells us that investing a dollar at the cost of capital yields a present value of a dollar and no new value is created. The firm simply gets bigger. This situation is typically accompanied by lagging knowledge-building proficiency that slows innovation in both process improvements and new products. Complacency with the status quo due to a sizable market share coupled to a large board of "don't rock the boat" directors sets the stage for the firm to transition to the failing business model stage (see Figure 3). Such a transition can typically take from five to 20 years, depending upon the competitive landscape.

Consider two scenarios for a firm such as Deere in the early 2000s with 50,000 employees. A successful transition (favorable fade) scenario can easily result in 75,000 *productive* employees 10 years later, while a decline to a failing business model stage can decimate the original 50,000 jobs. The 75,000 productive jobs should be compared to the large resources consumed by new startups, many of which fail in order that a few successful ones can eventually create 75,000 jobs. Concerning economic growth and job creation, it is myopic to solely focus in the extreme on startups while ignoring the corporate governance issues with large firms that can easily spiral downward. When the transition to the failing business model stage actually occurs, the lack of effective corporate governance causes a substantial misallocation and waste of resources over the five- to 20-year period until a major restructuring or bankruptcy occurs. Those resources could have been put to much more productive use, including job creation—a classic opportunity cost.

To the benefit of Deere's employees and shareholders, the firm transitioned over two decades via the favorable scenario. The first decade was under the CEO leadership of Robert Lane (2000-2009). Lane clearly understood Deere's position on its life-cycle track record. In a 2004 interview, Lane staked out Deere's fundamental challenge: "Over the past 40 years, there have only been spurts where we've actually even earned our cost of capital."[28] He understood that Deere's decentralized structure led to steady production in individual factories, but such *local optimization* turned out to be suboptimal for the firm as a whole operating in a highly cyclical business. Lane focused on upgrading Deere's knowledge-building proficiency, increasing the efficiency of work at all levels of the firm, boosting innovation and disciplined resource allocation.

How was knowledge-building proficiency upgraded in Deere's factories? Recall the emphasis on viewing the firm as a holistic system and avoiding analysis that isolates variables. The upgrading of Deere's knowledge-building proficiency was seen as an integral part of a culture transformation. That Deere's culture in its factories needed a radical overhaul was evident in the signs near the factory entrances enumerating shop rules, including "You will not assault a member of management." A detailed study of this transformation reveals that a culture of confrontation between union employees and factory managers was replaced with a shared vision; trust; respect for employees; win-win relationships (especially with union leaders); lean manufacturing; and training, mentoring, and teamwork to solve problems and reduce product defects. This culture transformation was also instrumental in improving work, innovation, and resource allocation in what has become a more holistic system.[29]

As a key part of this system, Lane implemented Deere's Shareholder Value Added (SVA) system to bring a quantitative discipline to guide improvements in operations and resource allocation. SVA is calculated as operating profit less an implied charge for capital. In Lane's words:

> We . . . hadn't really focused sufficiently on tightly managing our assets. So it was clear to me . . . that a simplified form of economic profit—focusing on the left-hand side of the balance sheet—would be just the ticket. My desire was to have something all of our operating people could embrace . . . something profound but very straightforward, intuitive, and simple.[30]

In his study of Deere's transformation, Mark Moran noted:

> Deere [under Lane's leadership] did several things to manage . . . SVA . . . Those include a disciplined R&D investment, global expansion, channel consolidation, channel expansion, domestic investment, and disciplined divestitures . . . a common language was required to make . . . salaried employees literate in what [operating return on assets] and SVA mean, how they are calculated, and how they measure the company's success.[31]

From 2010 to 2019, Sam Allen was Deere's CEO. Building on Lane's foundational improvements, the hallmark of Allen's tenure was superb execution, global expansion, and strategic acquisitions. In 2016, which was a down year for Deere's main agricultural business, Allen's shareholder letter highlights not only how Deere operates but also Deere's purpose. In a statement that rings true to the pragmatic theory's purpose of the firm, reinforcing a vision that aims to inspire and motivate employees to uphold the firm's commitment to ethical behavior and making the world a better place, Allen writes:

> Our ability to operate profitably throughout the business cycle reflects the advances we've made controlling costs and

> running our company with a lean slate of productive assets . . . SVA is the primary measure used in managing the company and making investment decisions . . . [strategy] continues to carry the theme of "feet on the ground, eyes on the horizon" and remains focused on meeting the needs of a growing, more affluent, and more urbanized population . . . Deere is committed to becoming the industry's undisputed leader in precision agriculture.
>
> Regardless of the changes needed to reach our goals, John Deere's commitment to how we do business is not subject to revision or reconsideration. Our core values—integrity, quality, commitment and innovation—have sustained the loyalty of generations of customers and are a source of inspiration for thousands of talented employees, dealers, and suppliers. Further, these values have supported business performance that has led to solid returns for our investors over many years.

The company's success is rooted in a long-term perspective that lays the economic facts on the table in terms of the firm's life-cycle track record (Figure 4). The pragmatic theory is about long-term value creation and, when applied to Deere, reveals that management made key decisions consistent with the four-part purpose of the firm, which includes win-win relationships with all of the firm's stakeholders. Nevertheless, those who have little interest in finance issues often dismiss SVA as a tool for boosting short-term profits solely for the benefit of shareholders even if it involves closing factories.

But this view is misguided.

Divesting businesses, selling assets that are worth more to someone else, and closing factories that don't justify reinvestment are an integral part of allocating resources to new projects capable of earning at least cost-of-capital returns. This is necessary in order for the firm to survive and prosper over the long term. When a firm sustains a knowledge-building culture, employees continually improve their problem-solving skills so that they can more easily transition to different jobs. If a factory has to be shut down, management has a responsibility to assist employees in securing new jobs, preferably elsewhere in the firm.

Also, the claim that SVA is short-term focused misses the life-cycle perspective and the need to avoid the failing business model stage. Consider how taking care of future generations through environmental sustainability initiatives is impacted when a firm with a failing business model and cash flow problems is forced to cut back on discretionary spending for environmental projects. Deere has sought to avoid this predicament by using some of its robust profits to fund huge R&D innovation designed to supply products and services with advanced technology that optimizes farmers' outputs by minimizing inputs and negative environmental impacts. This is truly a sustainable path to the benefit of the environment—and farmers' productivity, and of course, people who need nutritious and affordable food. For corporate critics concerned about companies shortchanging stakeholders by elevating shareholder returns, the long-term perspective held out by the pragmatic theory of the firm should be reassuring.

Intangible assets, shareholder returns, and three levels of cause-and-effect logic

When non-depreciable expenditures are incurred that provide benefits beyond the accounting period being measured, these expenditures represent intangible assets. Examples include the platforms of Amazon and Netflix for helping customers, lean manufacturing processes, brand-building outlays, employee education and training, and R&D expenditures. Increasingly in the New Economy, intangibles are involved with generating performance that yields, in life-cycle terms, long-term favorable fade and excess positive shareholder returns. Leading Old Economy firms scaled physical (tangible) assets, thereby gaining efficiency and market share. Leading New Economy firms scale up their platforms by connecting more and more users. Uber's business model depends upon avoiding tangible assets, since drivers own their own vehicles, and scaling up both its drivers and the consumers who use the Uber app on their cellphones.

Tangible assets, such as an office building or a fleet of trucks, typically have a value that is not dependent upon, and exists apart from, a firm. Not so for intangible assets that are an integral part of a business system that generates future cash flows. For example, an explicit estimate of a brand value can misleadingly imply a stand-alone value that can be obtained independently of the firm currently using the brand. All else equal, highly skilled management will utilize a brand much better than less-skilled management and generate higher future cash flows. For example, Daimler-Benz acquired control of Chrysler in 1998. The subsequent dismal financial performance reflected a lack of skill by Daimler-Benz management in both combining operations and utilizing the Chrysler brand. Chrysler was sold in 2007. Investors calculating warranted values for a firm based on different future scenarios can account for a brand's contribution to future financial performance via different fade forecasts of economic returns—the more valuable the brand, the more favorable the fade forecast.

So, the economy has changed and complexity has increased with the rise of intangible assets. But ask yourself, what if anything has remained unchanged about economic progress in both the New Economy and the Old Economy? The answer: value creation depends upon knowledge-building proficiency—the quality of ideas matters much more than growth in business-as-usual products and services. Certainly, the standard of living and job creation increased far more from introducing the automobile than from merely expanding capacity to produce horse-drawn carriages. Ideas were no less important in the Old Economy than they are in the New Economy. Ideas about internal combustion engines led to greater demand for oil reserves and the building of refineries. Such tangible assets had verifiable economic lives that translated into reliable accounting depreciation schedules enabling GAAP income statements and balance sheets to be highly useful for management, investors, institutions involved with credit and debt instruments, and regulators.

Intangible assets involve considerable uncertainty about the magnitude and duration (accounting life) of future benefits. Consequently, accounting rule-makers have been extraordinarily slow in adopting rules for capitalization and amortization of intangibles. In addition, both management and accounting firms lack incentives to put intangibles on the balance sheet. Management wants to avoid having to explain future write-offs of intangibles, possibly due to technological obsolescence. And accounting firms see future liabilities associated with their process for handling hard-to-value assets.[32]

The stock market doesn't wait for accounting rule-makers to assist with the analysis of intangibles. Considerable empirical research has documented the economically consequential link between intangible assets and stock prices.[33] Is the pragmatic theory useful for thinking about approaches to empirical research on shareholder returns in the New Economy? To answer that question, let's focus on three levels of cause-and-effect logic as to what drives a firm's market valuation.

Level 1 includes correlation studies, typically using readily available Compustat variables. These variables rarely contain a new insight that links a firm's financial performance and valuation over a firm's life cycle due to limited concern for how the growing importance of intangibles (not part of GAAP accounting) distorts Compustat-derived variables, such as book/price. The thrust of this research is to improve multi-factor models of risk and return. More than 300 factors have been reported in journal articles, leading to one characterization of this output as the "factor zoo."[34]

Furthermore, Level 1 studies are concerned neither with a deeper understanding of firms through a life-cycle analysis, nor with the importance of a firm's knowledge-building proficiency. For example, research has documented a negative correlation between excess shareholder returns and asset growth rates. Specifically, low asset growth firms earn higher shareholder returns, on average, than high asset growth firms.[35] However, a more fine-grained analysis would segment the data to ascertain the impact of knowledge-building proficiency in sustaining above-average profitability. Couple that with high asset growth rates and one would expect to observe positive excess returns. This line of thinking suggests that knowledge-building proficiency reflected in securing patents coupled with high asset growth rates may well lead to positive excess returns.[36]

Compared to Level 1, Level 2 studies display a heightened concern for cause-and-effect logic between a variable and its hypothesized impact on firm performance. If investors fail to appreciate a variable's importance for improving, or sustaining, a firm's profitability, they should at least be expected to raise a company's share value (producing excess positive returns) as the unexpected results are delivered.

Along with R&D expenditures, the next major source of investment that creates intangibles are those items in a firm's selling, general, and administrative (SG&A) expenditures that produce future benefits beyond the accounting period being measured. Research has demonstrated that decomposing SG&A expenditures into pure operating expenses versus expenses that are properly classified as intangible assets leads to improved predictability of future earnings and shareholder returns.[37] SG&A research is closer to practical use for management compared to Level 1 studies. For example, research has shown that after management received long-term equity incentives, corporate spending on those SG&A components tied to future economic benefits increased.[38]

Environmental, social, and governance (ESG) practices are receiving increased attention from large owners of publicly traded firms. This comports with the pragmatic theory's emphasis on firm purpose, including win-win relationships and taking care of future generations. A matched sample of firms with high-rated ESG practices versus low-rated showed that the former outperformed the latter over the long term both in terms of shareholder returns and accounting-based performance.[39] This result has frequently been replicated in other studies.[40] A legitimate concern is that management may spend resources excessively in order to secure a high rating on ESG scorecards and lose sight of the cost-of-capital discipline. The recent rapid growth of investment funds tailored to invest in highly rated ESG firms could contribute to such a misallocation of resources.

Level 3 studies are consistent with the pragmatic theory of the firm's emphasis on knowledge-building proficiency (high/low) as the fundamental cause of what shows up as long-term, excess (positive/negative) shareholder returns. Lauren Cohen, Karl Diether, and Christopher Malloy used a firm's track record of success in translating R&D expenditures into sales as a proxy for a firm's knowledge-building proficiency:

> Our approach is based on the simple idea that some firms are likely to be skilled at certain activities, and some are not, and this skill may be persistent over time. . . . We show that . . . substantial return predictability exists by exploiting the information in these firm-level track records. We find that a long-short portfolio strategy that takes advantage of the information in past track records yields abnormal returns of 11 percent per annum. . . . We show that the firms we classify

> as high ability based on their past track records also produce tangible results with their research and development efforts. In particular, R&D spending by high ability firms leads to increased numbers of patents, patent citations, and new product innovations by these firms in the future. The same level of R&D investments by low ability firms does not.[41]

Here is an important Level 3-type research question concerning firms that implement Lean principles. Why do only approximately 5% to 7% of firms that implement "lean" principles actually sustain superior performance over the long term? A useful, empirically based answer to this question is important not only to investors but most certainly to management.

A researcher working with this question would benefit from the experiences documented by Mark Deluzio, the principal architect of the Danaher Business System (DBS), which propelled Danaher to become the generally acknowledged preeminent "lean" firm in the U.S. In his book, *Flatlined: Why Lean Transformations Fail and What to Do About It,* Deluzio provides insights that are well suited for empirical research as to why Lean transformations fail. Of particular importance to a successful Lean transformation is full-time engagement by top management. Reinforcing the idea that employee education and training is an SG&A expense that should be treated as an intangible asset, Deluzio describes the DBS office that he managed:

> At Danaher, we also used the DBS office to train future leaders in our DBS methodology. Presidents and vice presidents, as well as other leaders, came out of their respective roles and worked full-time in the DBS office, anywhere from 6 to 12 months. When they returned to their line or staff role, they led DBS in their line role of their organization with almost

a religious fervor. Ultimate career success at Danaher was contingent upon one's ability to lead and achieve results utilizing the Danaher Business System.[42]

Concluding thoughts

The pragmatic theory of the firm offers an advantageous way of thinking about corporate purpose and success that can be distilled into four key points:

- Clarity about the purpose of the firm suggests that maximizing shareholder value is best viewed not as the firm's purpose, but as the result of the firm successfully achieving its four-part purpose.
- The pragmatic theory of the firm holistically treats the firm as a system of connected components rooted in the firm's purpose and utilizes a life-cycle framework. Life-cycle track records make sense of shareholder returns over time. When used to display the long-term performance of individual business units, life-cycle track records can help management and boards improve their resource allocation decisions.[43]
- The key determinant of the firm's long-term performance is its knowledge-building proficiency relative to its competitors'.
- Firm risk consists of obstacles to achieving the firm's purpose and involves not only controls to avoid bad (value destruction) experiences, but also a way of working that generates opportunities for good (value creation) experiences. Build knowledge to better manage firm risk, achieve favorable fade, and create long-term value.

The ongoing worldwide indictment of capitalism and the related criticism of corporate governance suggests that maximizing shareholder value is both easily misunderstood and ill-suited to gather broad support for the role of business firms in society. The pragmatic theory of the firm responds to this criticism with two main points.

- Human capital is spotlighted as the means to advance the firm's knowledge-building proficiency which is key to achieving the firm's four-part purpose—vision, survive and prosper, win-win relationships, and taking care of future generations. This four-part purpose addresses the core concerns of stakeholder capitalism while not neglecting that, for a firm to survive and prosper over the long term, it needs to earn at least the cost of capital.
- The pragmatic theory of the firm lays out an intellectual basis for management and the board to adopt a holistic view of the firm in order to make better value creation decisions to the long-term benefit of all stakeholders. Such decisions are rooted in constructive skepticism about key business assumptions; feedback to facilitate early adaptation to a fast-changing world; and investments in intangible assets that nurture and sustain a knowledge-building culture.

NOTES

[1] Bartley J. Madden. 2021. "The Pragmatic Theory of the Firm." *Journal of Applied Corporate Finance*. 33(1): 98-110.

[2] Alfred D. Chandler, "Organizational Capabilities and the Economic History of the Industrial Enterprise," *Journal of Economic Perspectives* 6(3) 1992, 79-100.

[3] Ronald Coase, "The Nature of the Firm: Origin, Meaning, Influence," *Journal of Law, Economics & Organization* 4(1) 1988: 3-47.

[4] Ronald Coase, "The Nature of the Firm," *Economica* 4(16) 1937: 386-405; Edith Penrose, *The Theory of the Firm* (Oxford: Oxford University Press, 1959); Richard M. Cyert and James G. Marsh, *A Behavioral Theory of the Firm* (Englewood Cliffs, NJ: Prentice Hall, 1963); Michael C. Jensen and William H. Meckling, "Theory of the Firm: Managerial Behavior, Agency Costs, and Ownership Structure," *Journal of Financial Economics* 3(4) 1976: 305-360; Oliver E. Williamson, "The Economics of Organizations: The Transaction Cost Approach," *American Journal of Sociology* 87(3) 1981: 548-577; Richard R. Nelson and Sidney G. Winter, *An Evolutionary Theory of Economic Change* (Cambridge, MA: Harvard University Press, 1982); Sanford Grossman and Oliver Hart, "The Costs and Benefits of Ownership: A Theory of Vertical and Lateral Integration," *Journal of Political Economy* 94(4) 1986: 691-719; Jay B. Barney, "Is the Resource-Based 'View' a Useful Perspective for Strategic Management Research? Yes," *Academy of Management Review* 26(1) 2001: 41-56; Bart Nooteboom, *A Cognitive Theory of the Firm: Learning, Governance and Dynamic Capabilities* (Northampton, MA: Edward Elgar, 2009); David J. Teece, "Knowledge Assets, Capabilities, and the Theory of the Firm," Chapter 23 in Mark Easterly-Smith and Marjorie A. Lyles, Eds. *Handbook of Organizational Learning and Knowledge Management* (Hoboken, NJ: John Wiley & Sons, 2011).

[5] Bartley J. Madden, *Value Creation Principles: The Pragmatic Theory of the Firm Begins with Purpose and Ends with Sustainable Capitalism* (Hoboken, NJ: John Wiley & Sons, 2020).

[6] Though I discuss work, innovation, and resource allocation at length in my cited 2020 book, I do not do so in this article.

[7] Bartley J. Madden, "Management's Key Responsibility," *Journal of Applied Corporate Finance* 30(3) 2018: 27-35.

[8] Robert M. Grant, "Toward a Knowledge-Based Theory of the Firm," *Strategic Management Journal* 17 (Winter Special Issue) 1996: 109-122.

[9] Mark C. Ubelhart, "An Economic View of the Impact of Human Capital on Firm Performance and Valuation," in Rawley Thomas and Benton E. Gup, Eds. *The Valuation Handbook: Valuation Techniques from Today's Top Practitioners* (Hoboken, NJ: John Wiley & Sons, 2010) pp. 508-524.

[10] Bartley J. Madden, "Management's Worldview: Four Critical Points about Reality, Language, and Knowledge Building," *Journal of Organizational Computing and Electronic Commerce* 22(4) 2012: 334-346.

[11] Rita McGrath, *Seeing Around Corners: How to Spot Inflection Points in Business* (Boston: Houghton Mifflin Harcourt, 2019) pp. 51-52 and 56.

[12] Chris Firth, *Making Up the Mind: How the Brain Creates Our Mental World* (Hoboken, NJ: John Wiley & Sons, 2007).

[13] For insights about the pioneering work of John Dewey and Adelbert Ames Jr. concerning our participation in shaping what we experience as reality, see Bartley J. Madden, "A Transactional Approach to Economic Research," *Journal of Socio-Economics* 20(1) 1991: 57-71. This article includes a criticism of Milton Friedman's methodology of positive economics. Both the article and Friedman's response are available at http://LearningWhatWorks.com/news.htm. For a comprehensive argument that behavioral economists and cognitive psychologists have underappreciated how individuals participate in creating their perceptions, see Teppo Felin, Jan Koenderink, and Joachim I. Krueger, "Rationality, Perception, and the All-Seeing Eye," *Psychon. Bull. Rev.*, published online: 7 December 2016.

[14] Lera Boroditsky, "How Language Shapes Thought: The languages we speak affect our perceptions of the world," *Scientific American*, February 2012. pp. 62-65.

[15] James F. Cox III and John G. Schleier, Jr., Eds. *Theory of Constraints Handbook* (New York: McGraw-Hill, 2010).

[16] Jim Womack, 2nd edition, *Gemba Walks* (Cambridge, MA: Lean Enterprise Institute, 2013).

[17] Frances A. Kennedy and Sally K. Widener, "A control framework: Insights from evidence on lean accounting," *Management Accounting Research* 19(4) 2008: 301-323.

[18] Clayton M. Christensen, Taddy Hall, Karen Dillon, and David S. Duncan, *Competing Against Luck: The Story of Innovation and Customer Choice* (New York: Harper Business, 2016).

[19] Brad Smith, "The Most Important Job of a CEO," Investors.Intuit.com, accessed March 13, 2016.

[20] Matthew S. Olson, Derek van Bever, and Seth Verry, "When Growth Stalls," *Harvard Business Review* March 86(3) 2008: 50-61.

[21] David R. Koenig, *The Board Member's Guide to Risk* (Northfield, MN: (b)right governance publications, 2020) pp. vii and 65.

[22] John A. Allison, *The Financial Crisis and the Free Market Cure: Why Pure Capitalism Is the World Economy's Only Hope* (New York: McGraw-Hill, 2013) p. 241.

[23] Indeed, Dave Denis argues that, based on his survey of relevant studies, corporate overinvestment appears to be a far more pervasive problem than corporate underinvestment. See David J. Denis, "Is Managerial Myopia a Persistent Governance Problem?" *Journal of Applied Corporate Finance* 31(3) 2019: 74-80.

[24] Luke Timmerman, "DNA Sequencing Market Will Exceed $20 Billion, Says Illumina CEO Jay Flatley," *Forbes*, April 29, 2015.

[25] For an updated technical explanation of CFROI, see David A. Holland and Bryant A. Matthews, *Beyond Earnings: Applying the HOLT CFROI and Economic Profit Framework* (Hoboken, NJ: John Wiley & Sons, 2018).

[26] The inflation-adjusted cost of capital for U.S. public companies generally was estimated at 5.95% in Eugene F. Fama and Kenneth R. French's "The Corporate Cost of Capital and the Return on Corporate Investment," *Journal of Finance* 54(6) 1999: 1939-1967.

[27] More research is needed focused on management decision-making when faced with a failing business model. See the analysis of Smith Corona's eventual bankruptcy and NCR's successful restructuring in my book cited earlier, *Value Creation Principles: The Pragmatic Theory of the Firm Begins with Purpose and Ends with Sustainable Capitalism*, pp. 194-198.

[28] Jeremy Grant, "Deere learns to handle difficult cycles," *Financial Times*, December 8, 2004. p. 30.

[29] Fred Stahl, *Worker Leadership: America's Secret Weapon in the Battle for Industrial Competitiveness* (Cambridge, MA: MIT Press, 2013). This book describes the crucial role of Dick Kleine in transforming Deere's culture one factory at a time while also laying the groundwork for a firmwide, substantially improved production process. The fundamental changes provide a model for utilizing human resources to the benefit of all stakeholders.

[30] Rodger Boehm, "Leading Change—An Interview with the CEO of Deere & Company," *McKinsey Quarterly*, December 2006.

[31] Mark Moran, "Not your grandfather's tractor company—transformation of the John Deere enterprise," *Journal of Enterprise Transformation*, 7(1-2) 2017: 40-73.

[32] Baruch Lev, "Ending the Accounting-for-Intangibles Status Quo," *European Accounting Review* 28(1) 2018: 1-24.

[33] Anne Wyatt, "What Financial and Non-financial Information on Intangibles Is Value Relevant? A Review of the Evidence," *Accounting and Business Research* 38(3) 2008: 217-256. For a comprehensive review, see Daniel Zeghal and Anis Maaloul, "The Accounting Treatment of Intangibles—A Critical Review of the Literature," *Accounting Forum* 35(4) 2011: 262-274.

[34] Campbell R. Harvey and Yan Liu, "Lucky Factors," available at SSRN: https://ssrn.com/abstract=2528780, August 7, 2020.

[35] Michael J. Cooper, Huseylin Gulen, and Michael J. Schill, "Asset Growth and the Cross-Section of Stock Returns," *Journal of Finance* 63(4) 2008: 1609-1651.

[36] Praveen Kumar and Dongmei Li, "Capital Investment, Innovative Capacity, and Stock Returns," *Journal of Finance* 71(5) 2016: 2059-2094.

[37] Luminita Enache and Anup Srivastava, "Should Intangible Investments Be Reported

Separately or Commingled with Operating Expenses?" *Management Science* 64(7) 2018: 3446-3468. Also, Annette Ptok, Rupinder P. Jindal, and Werner Reinartz, "Selling, General, and Administrative (SG&A) Expense-Based Metrics in Marketing: Conceptual and Measurement Challenges," *Journal of Academy of Marketing Science* 46(6) 2018: 987-1011.

[38] Ragiv Banker, Rong Huang, and Ram Natarajan, "Equity Incentives and Long-Term Value Created by SG&A Expenditures," *Contemporary Accounting Research* 28(3) 2011: 794-830.

[39] Robert G. Eccles, Ionnis Ioannou, and George Serafeim, "The Impact of Corporate Sustainability on Organizational Processes and Performance," *Management Science* 60(11) 2014: 2835-2857.

[40] Gordon L. Clark, Andreas Feiner, and Michael Viehs, *From the Stockholder to the Stakeholder* (Smith School of Enterprise and the Environment and Arabesque Partners, 2015). Also, Gunnar Friede, Timo Busch, and Alexander Bassen, "ESG and Financial Performance: Aggregated Evidence from More Than 2000 Empirical Studies," *Journal of Sustainable Finance & Investments* 5(4) 2015: 210-233.

[41] Lauren Cohen, Karl Diether, and Christopher Malloy, "Misvaluing Innovation," *Review of Financial Studies* 26(3) 2013: 635-666. Also, for a creative study that investigated the value of knowledge contributed by individuals, see Aaron K. Chatterji and Karl R. Fabrizio, "Does the Market for Ideas Influence the Rate and Direction of Innovative Activity? Evidence from the Medical Device Industry," *Strategic Management Journal* 37(3) 2016: 447-465.

[42] Mark C. Deluzio, *Flatlined: Why Lean Transformations Fail and What to Do About It* (New York: Routledge, 2020). The 5% to 7% figure is from the foreword written by Art Byrne, former CEO of Wiremold and an acknowledged Lean expert.

[43] Bartley J. Madden, "For Better Corporate Governance, the Shareholder Value Review," *Journal of Applied Corporate Finance* 19(1) 2007: 102-114. Also, Mark L. Frigo and Bartley J. Madden, "Strategic Life-Cycle Analysis: The Role of the CFO," *Strategic Finance*, October 2020, pp. 33-39.

CHAPTER 5

Journal of Applied Corporate Finance[1]

BET ON INNOVATION, NOT ESG METRICS, TO LEAD THE NET ZERO TRANSITION

Bartley J. Madden

In 1987, the United Nations defined sustainable development as meeting the needs of present generations without compromising the needs of future generations. Today, the top priority for sustainability is the transition to Net Zero—that is, net zero greenhouse gas (GHG) emissions. Carbon dioxide, a GHG, is a major contributor to global warming.

In the pages that follow, I provide three different perspectives on how companies are most likely to help get us to Net Zero. The first is the widespread, conventional perspective that Environmental, Social, and Governance (ESG) metrics will lead the way to a successful transition to Net Zero. The second uses systems thinking to better describe the complexity of navigating a path to Net Zero and highlights the critical role of innovation. The third promotes systems thinking for corporate boards with the aim of improving decision-making and accelerating innovation and adaptation in a fast-changing Net Zero world.

Perspective #1—ESG metrics

Facing pressure from institutional asset managers, companies today must begin navigating a path to Net Zero.[2] As metrics keyed to the "E" of ESG and specifically related to GHG emissions proliferate, investors are increasingly using ESG scorecards as part of their decision-making. At the beginning of 2022, the capital devoted to exchange-traded, ESG-focused funds exceeded $2.7 trillion. Moreover, regulatory bodies continue to make this kind of data mandatory in corporate reports. As a consequence, managements and boards of directors are motivated to take actions that can make their companies look good at least in terms of ESG metrics.

But the objective of such companies ought, of course, to be to reduce their GHG emissions. The current default reporting methodology is the GHG Protocol, in accord with which Scope 1 emissions are those directly produced by a firm's operations—for example, from driving owned and leased vehicles. Scope 2 missions are those produced by facilities that generate electricity bought and consumed by the company. Scope 3 emissions originate from upstream operations in a company's supply chain and from downstream use by both its "wholesale" and end-use consumers. The GHG Protocol methodology has been criticized as lacking accuracy and verifiability (primarily in terms of Scope 3), in significant part for requiring that the same emissions reported multiple times by different companies.

To address this and other limitations of the Protocol, Robert Kaplan and Karthik Ramanna have proposed an innovative solution that recognizes the integrated nature of pollution activities across the economy. A company's existing accounting system and cost-accounting infrastructure would record the GHG units emitted during operations as an *E-liability*.[3] All along the supply chain, companies would transfer the E-liability associated with goods delivered and record their end-of-period E-liability. This method eliminates multiple counting of emissions in the conceptually flawed Stage 3 method while also limiting opportunities for greenwashing gamesmanship.

The conventional perspective with its emphasis on ESG metrics represents linear cause-and-effect thinking. That is, a logically tight path is assumed to exist from implementing ESG metrics to "incentivizing" companies to take actions to improve their ESG scores, eventually leading to a successful Net Zero transition. Interestingly, those who embrace this perspective invariably do appreciate the complexity and messiness of the climate change problem reflected in the interrelatedness that brings together political, economic, ecological, and social issues with multiple causes generating multiple effects often separated in time and space.[4]

Linear cause-and-effect thinking frequently leads to the promotion of overly simplistic means to achieve goals. Why? Mainly because written and verbal communications are perceived as persuasive when key points are presented in a logically tight *linear* manner. Today's leaders frequently prefer confident conclusions to the tentativeness and epistemological humility exhibited by systems thinkers. Why not put systems thinking front and center since it facilitates the use of alternative ways of seeing the world that can overcome more narrow perceptual processes often driven by rigid and ossified assumptions?[5] To embrace systems thinking is to continually question key assumptions, to organize feedback (especially from experimentation), and to appreciate, and actively seek, diverse points of view; along with a *sustained curiosity* about mapping the intricacies of interrelationships in a complex system.[6] Such alternative perspectives can reveal faulty assumptions and lead to expedited learning that helps identify key constraints and leverage points in order to improve system performance. Easier said than done.

The linear cause-and-effect choice appears sensible to many because promoting a pure systems-thinking approach means a journey full of surprises and the need to adapt and deal with unforeseen problems, while making mistakes along the way as a necessary part of learning about system complexity. But some may perceive this as a journey to climb a mountain that has no top—that is, an integrated, holistic understanding of the climate system with all the interrelatedness with other systems. Hence, the preference to minimize future surprises and to take the easier route laid out by ESG metrics.

However, leading systems thinker Michael Jackson cautions those who opt for simplicity in dealing with our complex world:

> What help can decision-makers expect when tackling the "messes" and "wicked problems" that proliferate in this age of complexity? They are usually brought up on classical management theory that emphasizes the need to forecast, plan, organize, lead, and control. This approach relies on there being a predictable future environment in which it is possible to set goals that remain relevant into the foreseeable future; on enough stability to ensure that tasks arranged in a fixed hierarchy continue to deliver efficiency and effectiveness; on a passive and unified workforce; and on a capacity to take control action on the basis of clear measures of success. These assumptions do not hold in the modern world, and classical management theory provides the wrong prescriptions. . .managers are left to persevere with their favorite panacea. . .systems thinking [is] the only appropriate response to complexity.[7]

Interdependencies along the path to Net Zero

The interrelatedness of GHG emissions with geopolitical risk became readily apparent with Russia's invasion of Ukraine beginning in February 2022, coupled with the dependency of many European countries on imports of Russian oil, gas, and coal. European policy makers concerned with their energy security began reassessing their increased fossil fuel usage from non-Russian sources, including liquefied natural gas from the U.S. A related geopolitical risk is China's assertion of control over Taiwan. Under this scenario, those countries that actively oppose China could find their supply of Chinese rare earth minerals—those required for electrical vehicle batteries—suffering a long-term disruption.

Take lithium, which is a critical component of batteries. One of the world's largest deposits of lithium has been discovered in Nevada's Thacker Pass. A mining permit was issued in February 2022 after a lengthy battle with U.S. environmentalists who, notwithstanding their support for green energy are adamantly opposed to such mining in the U.S. They have filed additional lawsuits to stop this mining operation. Keep in mind that batteries for electric vehicles contain a witches' brew of metals—lithium, nickel, cobalt, copper, and rare earth metals such as neodymium and dysprosium. The current mining process results in substantial environmental degradation, which will only get worse thanks to accelerating demand. Nevertheless, U.S. mining of these metals—which means replacing a portion mined outside the U.S.—would entail highly regulated processes that, from a global system perspective, would yield a net environmental improvement and reduce the risk of supply disruptions for U.S. electric vehicle manufacturers.

Solar panels, wind turbines, battery-powered electric vehicles, and the retirement of coal-burning power plants are the face of decarbonization for the general public. The problem, however, is that such initiatives fall well short of what will be needed to achieve Net Zero. Complexities abound. Solar and wind are intermittent sources of electricity, needing to be transported over an old and inefficient electric grid. Plus their intermittency requires carbon dioxide-emitting natural gas powerplants (assuming declining nuclear and retired coal plants) to even out supply and demand. In addition, intermittent renewables do not address hard-to-electrify sectors like steel, cement, and air travel.

The promise of hydrogen

One ray of hope now comes from the growing global consensus that hydrogen may be able—and indeed perhaps necessary—to achieve Net Zero.[8] Thirty countries have announced hydrogen transition strategies. But in thinking about this possibility, let's start by considering some key technical details, the kind of thing that plays a critical role in systems thinking.

Hydrogen stores energy and offers a low-cost means for transport as a gas through pipelines and in liquified form via trucks and ships. Hydrogen can be blended with natural gas and delivered using many of today's existing natural gas pipelines. Most hydrogen is currently produced using natural gas.

But not all hydrogen is environmentally equal. If and when carbon dioxide is emitted as part of this process, the output is labeled grey hydrogen. Blue hydrogen is produced when the carbon dioxide is captured and not released into the atmosphere. And *green* hydrogen is produced from renewables.

Electrolyzers take in water and electricity to produce hydrogen gas as an output. One notable technical advancement with considerable promise has been developed by a U.S. company called Heliogen. Its closed-loop electrolyzer system continually adjusts mirrors to optimally direct sunlight as an energy source to generate cost-effective hydrogen without fossil fuels. Fuel cells are energy converters that take in hydrogen (or natural gas) and produce electricity as an output.

We can expect sharply declining prices for electrolyzers and fuel cells as hydrogen adoption accelerates. In the language of systems thinking, there would thus be a positive feedback loop. As to hydrogen-powered vehicles, the longer the trip and the heavier the vehicle, the more competitive they become versus electric battery-powered vehicles.

A further boost for hydrogen could come from hydrogen production using the small modular (nuclear) reactors (SMRs) now being developed in the U.S. by NuScale Power, TerraPower, and others. SMRs could power electrolyzers that generate hydrogen without emitting carbon dioxide.

In fact, SMRs are currently being considered as a possible replacement for coal-fired plants. And once the technology for electricity generated by SMRs has proven itself, the existing infrastructure could be used to deliver electricity. Also, the coal plant's employees could transition to operating the SMRs. Proponents of SMRs make a strong point when they note that total GHG emissions for solar, including those from production of solar panels, are four times that of nuclear.[9]

Marco Alvea, CEO of Snam, Europe's largest gas pipeline and storage company and hydrogen first-mover, summarizes the promise of hydrogen as follows:

> I realized that hydrogen's true mission was to help us harvest sunlight and wind where they were in plentiful supply, transport them cheaply, and get them into our airplanes, factories, and homes. Just 1% of the Sahara Desert gets enough sunlight to power the whole world, and hydrogen could finally give us a way to unlock that potential and decarbonize the hard-to-electrify sectors at the same time . . . There is a growing consensus that hydrogen could account for up to a quarter of our energy needs in 2050 . . . On land, highly

> compressed hydrogen offers long range and fast refueling. It could be the most effective fuel for trucks, buses and taxi fleets, and it may well compete with batteries for passenger cars, too.[10]

Businesses worldwide would be impacted by the hydrogen transition. Consider geopolitics and the gain in economic power by major exporters of hydrogen, including Australia, Chile, the Middle East, and North Africa. Major importers of hydrogen would include Japan, South Korea, and Central Europe. Finally, the economic leverage currently wielded by Russia would plummet in lockstep with a decline in its exports of oil, gas, and coal.

But having considered this one possibility, let's now take a step back before diving deeper into interrelated subsystems that comprise the emergent climate change system. Could there be a better starting point than ESG metrics for thinking about getting to Net Zero? What about the purpose of the firm itself?

Rethinking corporate purpose

Another promising application of systems thinking is what I have taken to calling the Pragmatic Theory of the Firm.[11] According to the theory, a company's success in maximizing shareholder value is likely to depend on its effectiveness in accomplishing four critical tasks:

- *Communication of a vision of the company and its social as well as economic mission* with the power to motivate and even inspire employees.
- *Continuous gains in efficiency and sustained innovation* that enable the company to provide operating returns that at least equal its cost of capital, which in turn depend on a firm's knowledge-building proficiency. No company can survive and prosper that fails to provide its investors with competitive returns.

- *Commitment to building and maintaining win-win relationships* with all of the firm's stakeholders.
- *Investment in the well-being of future generations.* Management and the board should commit the firm to making contributions to the sustainability of the environment that the firm is well-positioned to carry out, with particular attention to the design of products and manufacturing processes that aim to minimize waste and pollution, which again depends on a firm's knowledge-building proficiency.

The theory concludes with the recognition that a company's knowledge-building proficiency is the critical determinant of innovation that drives long-term performance and connects corporate operating performance to its market valuation via a life-cycle framework.

One advantage of this four-part conception of corporate purpose is its emphasis on the "four oars in the water" that need to work in unison to generate economic as well as social value and progress. Perhaps most important is the underscoring of the core message of finance: the imperative for corporate managements to earn at least its cost of capital—a message that often gets overlooked in discussions of plans to get to Net Zero. And as viewed through the lens of the Pragmatic Theory of the Firm, the Net Zero transition is also an integral part of corporate purpose, as is the critical role of the Circular Economy in eliminating waste (e.g., non-recyclable plastics).[12]

To sum up, then, corporate purpose should be seen as an integral part of a *causal mechanism* that we collectively intend to lead to economic and social progress on not just a national, but on a global scale. Progress for developed nations alone will not be enough; it must aim to work for all. And the message here is that better alignment of corporate strategy, organizational structure, compensation, culture, and governance with its four-part purpose may well be our best hope for improving long-term social as well as economic performance.[13] With this end in view, ESG and Corporate Social Responsibility (CSR) metrics, the triple bottom line, the Net Zero Economy, and the Circular Economy can and are being used to monitor companies' effectiveness in accomplishing aspects of their four-part purpose. Conspicuously absent from the UN's definition of sustainability is recognition of corporate innovation's role in *sustainable progress* (perhaps a more useful term than *sustainability*), the kind that generates the rising standard of living that is the surest means of improving the prospects of future generations. The virtue and promise of my four-part approach to corporate purpose is that it trains the spotlight directly on corporate innovation, which, together with execution of the strategy, end up being the main drivers of long-run corporate profitability and value.

Perspective #2—innovation is critical to achieving Net Zero

Complex systems are built on the premise of a world of great uncertainty, in which some possibly as yet unknown variables are almost *expected* to emerge ("we know something important is going to change, we just don't know what it will be"), thereby upsetting the plans of those who extrapolate the future based on what is known today.[14] When operating in such a world, management and boards should give top priority to monitoring innovation developments and ensuring they have adaptable plans for the Net Zero journey.[15]

We should expect companies that produce significant Net Zero innovations to include both out-of-the-box-thinking startups and established firms with proven capabilities, substantial financial resources, and motivation to lead the Net Zero transition. In his 2022 Blackrock Letter to CEOs, Larry Fink notes:

> The next 1000 unicorns won't be search engines or social media companies, they'll be sustainable, scalable innovators—startups that help the world decarbonize and make the energy transition affordable for all consumers. . . . With the unprecedented amount of capital looking for new ideas, incumbents need to be clear about their pathway to succeeding in a net zero economy. And it's not just startups that can and will disrupt industries. Bold incumbents can and must do it too. Indeed, many incumbents have an advantage in capital, market knowledge, and technical expertise on the global scale required for the disruption ahead.

Let's take a quick look at some of the Net Zero activities of three large established companies that have largely gone under the radar, unheralded if not actually scorned by ESG rating agencies. One is Honeywell, which currently receives an "F" overall grade for GHG disclosures/targets/reductions by As You Sow.[16] Another is Weyerhaeuser, which has become a timber REIT and not customarily viewed as a source of significant innovation. The third is Occidental Petroleum, a large oil producer certainly not revered by environmental activists.

Honeywell's businesses focus on aerospace, building technologies, performance materials and technologies, and safety and productivity solutions. Given the firm's deep knowledge of customer needs coupled to its innovation skill, you might expect that management's decision to commit 60% of its R&D budget to customer-ESG improvements would yield significant results. You would be right.

Here are a few highlights of important Honeywell innovations that advance Net Zero. The use of Honeywell's Solstice line of low global warming refrigerants, propellants, and solvents has resulted to date in the equivalent of removing 42 million cars from the road for 1 year. The company is also developing a green jet fuel that would replace petroleum jet fuel. Honeywell's green diesel fuel reduces GHG emissions by 80%, its unique flow battery technology is on a path to enable large-scale renewable energy storage, and its core business of control and automation of building and factory operations continues to enable its customers to attain higher-sustainability performance.

For 120 years, Weyerhaeuser has been growing, harvesting, and regrowing forests on a continuous cycle. Weyerhaeuser has historically been a sustainability leader, and is carbon negative by virtue of trees' absorption of carbon dioxide. The company meets 70% of its energy needs using renewable biomass. Weyerhaeuser is also well positioned to promote and seize a big opportunity for engineered "mass timber"—glued-together wooden pieces— to replace concrete and steel in new building construction. Along with lower construction costs and aesthetically pleasing buildings, GHG emissions are substantially reduced versus the status quo. Weyerhaeuser has also announced plans to lease portions of its 11 million acres of U.S. timberland for wind and solar production and to participate in the carbon offsets market.

The firm has a unique opportunity for high-ROI projects that use selected land parcels with the right geological formation to store carbon dioxide. As one example, Oxy Low Carbon Ventures, a subsidiary of Occidental Petroleum, will use Carbon Engineering's Direct Air Capture (DAC) technology on Weyerhaeuser land to capture and permanently sequester carbon dioxide from the atmosphere.[17] This planned one-million-ton annual capacity plant will be the world's biggest DAC facility, and aerospace leader Airbus has signed up for 400,000 tons of carbon-removed credits.

From a corporate finance valuation perspective, Occidental Petroleum's challenge is also an opportunity and one that all large oil and gas companies now face. If we view the firm's current market value as the sum of the net present value of existing assets and future investments, then one can "back out" the implied value of future investments by subtracting the estimated value of its current, established operations from today's known total market value of equity plus debt. But when one does this calculation, whether for Oxy or most of the majors, one finds a value for future investments that is substantially negative, indicating that investors are forecasting ROIs on future investments to be well below the cost of capital.

The flip side of this problem is the opportunity for the majors to gain substantial market value by giving investors reasons to forecast ROIs at least equal to the cost of capital on future capital expenditures. The key here is to be making new investments that can meet the cost-of-capital criterion at scale—new, big market opportunities. These opportunities exist in hydrogen, SMRs, carbon capture and storage, hard-to-decarbonize sectors, and new ways to use carbon dioxide and so avoid releasing it in the atmosphere. Occidental Petroleum is investing in most of these areas while aiming to take advantage of its core competency in carbon dioxide management. The above-mentioned DAC plant is one example.

To sum up, the rate of progress in getting to Net Zero critically depends upon innovation at the firm level; specifically, how management adapts and leverages existing capabilities to seize Net-Zero-related opportunities for innovation. Hence, a deeper understanding of how companies create value in today's economy can provide a lens to better see Net Zero progress at ground level, as opposed to high-level goals for GHG emissions and related ESG metrics. That lens has two components. First is greater appreciation of the New Economy that has spawned ecosystems that increasingly offer a path to shared value. Second are insights about long-run corporate performance in relation to the all-important cost-of-capital criterion that come from viewing companies with the life-cycle framework I say more about below.

The new economy and ecosystems

The New Economy is often described as the steady growth in the importance and value of intangible assets in relation to the tangible assets recorded on accounting statements. As one example, the power of platforms and networks is well documented as a major value-creating part of the New Economy. In addition, a company's performance is increasingly impacted by business ecosystems. James Moore foresaw the importance of ecosystems as early as 1993, when he wrote:

> Successful businesses are those that evolve rapidly and effectively. Yet innovative businesses can't evolve in a vacuum. They must attract resources of all sorts, drawing in capital, partners, suppliers, and customers to create cooperative networks . . . I suggest that a company be viewed not as a member of a single industry but as part of a *business ecosystem* that crosses a variety of industries. In a business ecosystem, companies co-evolve capabilities around a new innovation. They work cooperatively and competitively to support new products, satisfy customer needs, and eventually incorporate the next round of innovations.[18]

Business ecosystems are communities or networks of companies continually learning how to exploit enhanced connectivity both to collaborate and compete in value-creating ways not possible by standalone firms. A firm that creates and orchestrates the advancement of an ecosystem may secure sustained competitive advantage. Ecosystems have the capacity to evolve in surprising ways. For ecosystems, systems thinking is more useful than traditional linear cause-and-effect thinking.

Ecosystems can be classified as problem solution or transaction facilitation. The Apple iPhone initially originated as a solution ecosystem that coordinated app developers, telecom providers, and firms supplying components. Later Apple's App Store facilitated the purchase of apps. Meanwhile, reminiscent of Old Economy thinking, the BlackBerry phone rapidly lost market share with its focus on data security while paying minimal attention to the needs of app developers.

Discovery is an insurance company based in South Africa whose mission is to make people healthier and protect and enhance their lives through its life and health insurance policies. Management recognized the mutual benefits achievable by providing its customers with financial incentives to change their behavior in ways enabling them to lead longer and healthier lives. Skilled in behavioral economics and clinical science, Discovery uses apps and wearable fitness monitors to connect with customers in ways designed to motivate healthier lifestyles, including weight and exercise goals, and healthier food. The firm's large and expanding database is a gold mine for behavioral research to continually improve the healthy living process. The resulting ecosystem includes suppliers of healthy food, exercise facilities, and other insurance firms now partnering with Discovery.

Today, there are industries in which competitors need to march arm-in-arm and build *for-the-greater-good ecosystems.*[19] Food retailers have joined such an ecosystem—the Global Food Safety Initiative—with the shared understanding that food safety should never become a competitive advantage.

Countries have succeeded in collaborating by means of such greater-good ecosystems to make progress on especially difficult challenges far more productively than working independently.[20]

One case in point is the potential usefulness of a carbon price—a price per ton of carbon dioxide equivalent gas emitted.

The main alternative to the use of carbon prices is simply to set targets for emissions that apply to and are equally binding on all. The problem with such targets, however, is their failure to take account and make use of possibly significant differences in the costs incurred by companies and individuals in complying with such targets. By contrast, specification of a carbon price is designed to facilitate and get the greatest possible social benefit from economy-wide decision making that balances costs and benefits, including the use of less-carbon-intensive alternatives. Most economists agree that the carbon price should reflect the full social costs—that is, the total economic damage associated with each ton emitted. Although determining the optimal carbon price may require considerable experimentation and error, such a challenge is likely to appear trivial next to the implementation and enforcement challenges involved in the choice of the optimal regulatory limit on allowable emissions and the exceptions that are allowed in order to ensure sufficient fuel, heat, and light.

A global ecosystem focused on implementing a carbon price addresses the free-rider problem in which politicians seek what they perceive to be in their own national interests. Solving this problem would be a significant—indeed perhaps the most significant—step toward achieving Net Zero. To help ensure workability, such an ecosystem could penalize nonparticipants with tariffs on non-participant exports to member countries. This kind of for-the-better-good ecosystem can overcome the free-rider dilemma at the root of why the voluntary commitments associated with the Paris Accord and the Kyoto Protocol have failed to work as intended.[21]

Managing in response to the realities of the corporate life cycle

Figure 1 illustrates the transitional stages in the life cycle of corporate profitability and growth that all companies can expect to experience. As discussed above and depicted in Figure 1, more and more companies operate in environments that increasingly make use of ecosystems.

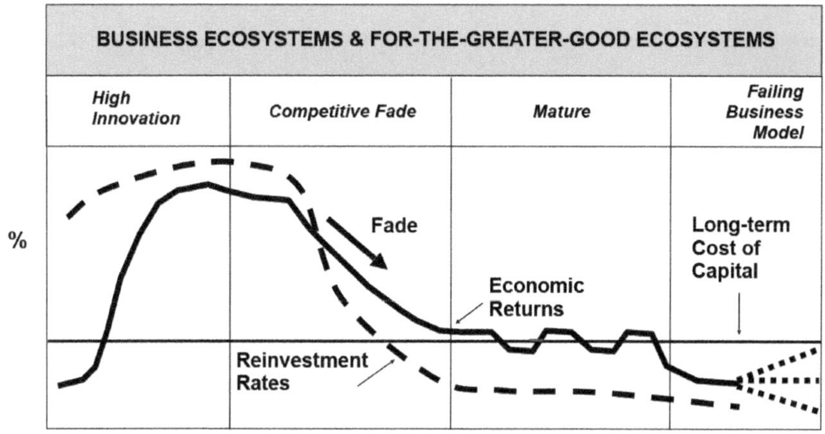

Figure 1. The Life-Cycle Framework

During the *high-innovation* stage, management of a startup needs quickly to either confirm or discard its core business model assumptions. Economic returns on invested capital that are well above the cost of capital are the hallmark of a business model's successful commercialization. For businesses that can scale, high reinvestment rates will be observed. Other firms are motivated to duplicate and improve upon a successful startup's business model, especially when high reinvestment rates indicate a big market opportunity.

During the *competitive fade* stage that follows, economic returns fall back towards the cost of capital, and the reinvestment rates, reflecting organic growth, fade towards an economy-type growth rate. A management that delivers sustained economic returns well above the cost of capital (favorable fade) typically has cemented a knowledge-building, pro-innovation culture coupled with win-win partnerships with all stakeholders. They continually build or acquire new capabilities that expand their firm's investment horizon.

Eventually, however, the firm enters the *mature* stage and earns approximately cost of capital returns and its reinvestment rates slow considerably. Management needs to adapt early to change and faces a tough task. The challenge is to continuously improve the efficiency of existing businesses while innovating in new areas that might even compete with business units that currently pay the bills.

One reliable signal of a firm entering the *failing business model* stage is a business-as-usual complacency with an attendant bureaucratic culture wherein the future is seen as a mirror image of the past. Guarding against and rooting out such a business-as-usual culture should be the top priority.

The case of Cummins

Management, boards of directors, and investors can benefit from using the life-cycle framework. With this end in mind, let's view the recent history of Cummins, a leading Net Zero innovator, using a life-cycle lens.

Cummins designs, manufactures, distributes, and services diesel, natural gas, electric, and hybrid powertrains and related components. The firm has the market leading position in diesel engines for trucks and other industrial applications. A better appreciation of the micro-innovation processes taking place at Cummins (see Figure 2) and other such companies can improve our understanding of how the global aggregate of these type of innovations ends up driving national and indeed global economic growth.[22]

As shown in the top panel, Cummins' economic returns are calculated as CFROIs—cash flow returns on investment that are adjusted for inflation and other biases (e.g., R&D outlays are capitalized rather than expensed).[23] Inflation adjustments are necessary to provide more accurate measures of levels and trends over long time periods. The benchmark, inflation-adjusted cost of capital is shown as a horizontal line at 6%.[24]

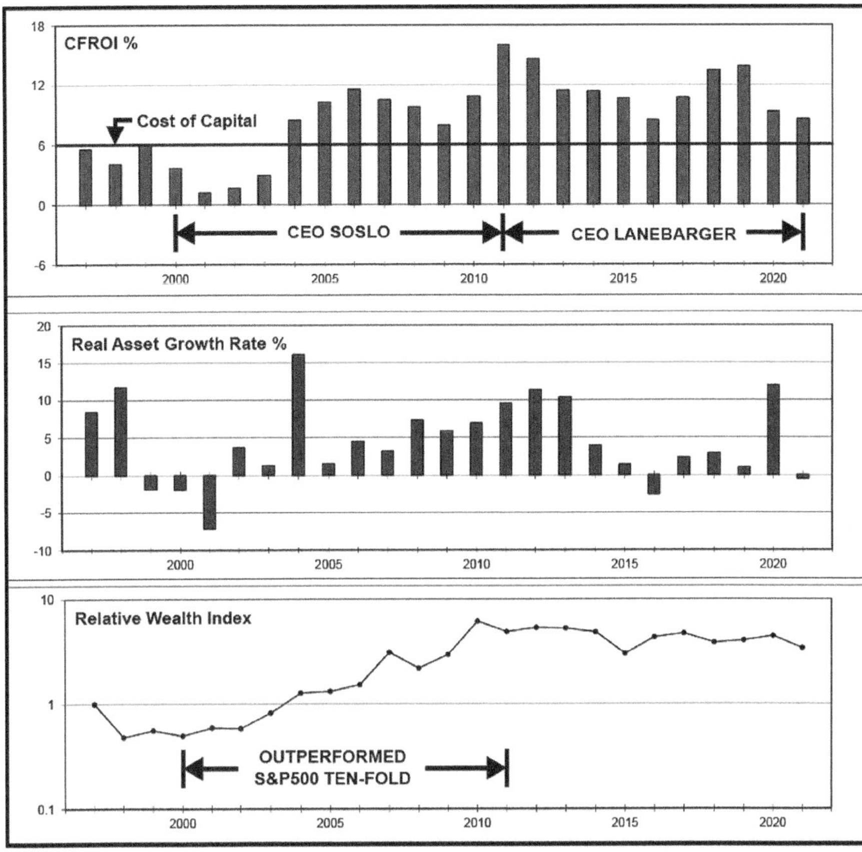

Figure 2. Cummins life cycle, 1997 to 2021
Source: Based on Credit Suisse HOLT global database

As can be seen in the figure, Cummins was losing market share for diesel engines as reflected in CFROIs at or below the cost of capital from 1997 to 2003. But when Tim Solso became CEO in 2000, he succeeded in systematically orchestrating productivity improvements while substantially increasing R&D outlays. Those R&D investments generated the innovations that enabled Cummins' diesel engines to meet new EPA emissions standards without compromising fuel efficiency—a significant competitive advantage.

Nevertheless, it took investors a while to recognize the structural changes that led to improvements in market share and profitability under Solso's leadership. As Figure 2 displays, Cummins' cyclical CFROIs surged above the cost of capital in 2004 and continued at that value-creating level while reinvestments rates (middle panel) remained solid. Thereafter, investors continually ratchetted up their expectations for favorable fade of future CFROIs. And during Solso's tenure from 2000 to 2011, Cummins stock outperformed the S&P 500 approximately 10-fold.

In sum, Soslo was building Cummins for the long term. He greatly expanded the firm's global footprint in the spirit of win-win partnerships. The hallmark of Cummins' foreign joint ventures has been the development of products specifically attuned to local markets and the development of local talent to assume leadership roles.

When Tom Linebarger succeeded Solso as CEO in 2012, he maintained the superior performance of his predecessor (see Figure 2 top panel). Based on the strategies he has implemented and the resource allocation decisions he has made, Linebarger can be described as a systems thinker *par excellence*. Systems thinkers appreciate how complex systems evolve in non-linear and hard-to-forecast ways. Because they understand the significant inaccuracies in forecasts of how complex systems will behave in the future, they avoid committing their organizations to dogmatic strategies that are ill-suited to a fast-changing world.

The complexity facing Cummins and other manufacturers is seen as a relatively new and emerging phenomenon: technologies compete by increasing efficiency and reducing costs, infrastructure develops, regulations change, and value as perceived by customers changes—all of which are interrelated and impacted by the pace of adoption of technology solutions. To no one's surprise, Linebarger has immersed Cummins in leading-edge technological developments with an eye on learning what technologies and related infrastructure will provide the best value for customers.

Of course, one should expect to continue to hear the incessant warnings that Tesla's electric-powered trucks (short haul and even long haul) are on the verge of displacing Cummins' dominant position in truck engines *because* electric is green. But this is likely to prove yet another instance of the fallibility of linear cause and effect thinking. The "electric is green" mantra ignores the emissions and environmental damage caused by the manufacturing of turbines, solar panels, and batteries themselves, not to mention the fossil-fuel-generated energy required to make up the inevitable shortfalls from intermittent wind and solar. And perhaps the main impetus for the most serious counter argument is likely to come from the 12 million owners of trucks powered by Cummins diesel engines who have already experienced the benefits from the company's stream of innovations. It's a matter of earned trust, which reflects the potential advantage of innovative incumbents noted earlier by Larry Fink. Cummins has a unique incumbent advantage that derives from its past services that provided a broad array of customers with diverse technologies—diesel, natural gas, propane, hydrogen, fuel cell, and battery systems.

In sum, Linebarger is positioning Cummins to be a leader in the Net Zero transition with a range of solutions tailored to customer needs. He has acquired firms with hydrogen, fuel cell, and battery expertise. The recent acquisition of Meritor, a leader in axle and brake technology, will facilitate the delivery of integrated powertrain solutions across combustion and electric power applications. The New Power division has been tasked with commercializing green alternatives to the existing diesel engine business. Meanwhile, the company's engineers continue to work to improve the efficiency of diesel engines, including the use of cleaner fuels such as hydrogen, as an integral part of the Net Zero transition. Notably, Cummins has achieved a series of firsts for significant hydrogen milestones: Florida's first green hydrogen plant using

Cummins electrolyzers; world's largest electrolyzer in Canada; Europe's first hydrogen-powered passenger train; the first large-scale hydrogen refueling station in Belgium; and the largest PEM (polymer electrolyte membrane) plant in the U.S.

Linebarger sums up his view of the Net Zero transition as follows: "I look at decarbonization and say that's a growth opportunity for Cummins, because now innovation is going to matter a lot. Innovation is what we do."[25] And the company's success accordingly illustrates the main message of this paper—that the real action in the Net Zero transition is taking place with innovation that can easily be missed, especially in the early stages, by ESG metrics. Game-changing innovation at the firm level is how society truly benefits from free-market capitalism.

But how has Cummins performed in terms of the previously discussed four-part corporate purpose? Cummins' *vision* of making people's lives better by powering a more prosperous world through innovation has proved inspiring to employees because their work is exactly about implementing this vision and, in so doing, making the world a better place. As to *surviving and prospering*, the substantial (and sustained) CFROI improvement to above-cost-of-capital level is both a testament to Cummins' innovation skill under Soslo and Linebarger, and the means to finance the investments required to accelerate the Net Zero transition. Cummins is widely respected for working to sustain *win-win relationships* with employees, customers, and other stakeholders. Finally, as to *taking care of future generations*, that is an apt description of the operating (how we do things) culture at Cummins.

The Net Zero world showcases a common denominator for firms of any size, ranging from high tech smaller firms like Heliogen with its innovative fossil-fuel-free electrolyzer and NuScale Power's small modular nuclear reactors to large firms like Cummins with a global and diverse customer base. As these examples all suggest, the Net Zero transition puts a premium on sustaining a knowledge-building culture that drives innovation and is central to achieving the firm's four-part purpose, which is the ultimate responsibility of the board of directors to which we now turn.

Perspective #3—boards of directors, systems thinking, and viability tests

The success of the Net Zero transition will depend heavily on boards' effectiveness in motivating, compensating, and monitoring management in ways consistent with long-term value creation, including sustaining a pro-innovation culture with potential to gain competitive advantage. There is little doubt that companies will develop new ways of reducing emissions from their internal processes. But one should expect such best practices to be widely implemented by industry competitors. Hence, no competitive advantage here. As suggested earlier, the big promise is almost certain to come from new, and as yet largely unrecognized, opportunities to earn ROIs well in excess of the cost of capital on large-scale capital outlays—opportunities that will be discovered in their products and services that are uniquely suited to meet customers' needs in the Net Zero world and are difficult for competitors to duplicate at the scale of the innovators. This is the story we have been telling about companies like Honeywell and Cummins.[26]

Compensation plans in shareholder proxy documents often contain *short-term* (3 years or less) plan horizons with no references to corporate returns or the cost of capital. But to repeat my earlier message, companies that consistently fail to earn the cost of capital will not survive as independent companies—and thus there will be no *long term*. Compensation plans should accordingly be designed as part of a company-wide financial management system focused on creating long-term value, not as an isolated document that compensation consultants craft with simplistic quartile rankings and short-term metrics and indicators.[27] Boards would benefit from having directors with systems thinking expertise. The more attention to systems thinking, the more apparent becomes the inadequacy of the information provided to boards, which is typically orchestrated by CEOs (especially when the CEO also serves as the board's chairperson).

Boards receive information that focuses principally on budgets, strategic reviews, resource allocations, and, in today's world, presumably plans to navigate the Net Zero transition. Michael Jensen has long made a strong case that boards need to control the flow of information required to fulfill their oversight responsibilities:

> The mindset of boards must move from one of careful review to one of insatiable curiosity. . . Question assumptions. . .Boards should take personal responsibility for understanding how traditional budget processes and stretch goals frequently inculcate a lack of integrity in an organization and destroy value . . . Rarely do board members have the kind of information they need to assess accurately the progress of the corporation. Getting that information requires boards to overhaul the process by which they get substantive information about corporate performance from one controlled by the CEO to one in which the board has ready access to relevant information.[28]

Consider an environment where the board is fully engaged with a management team that provides the information that the board believes is needed. What might that look like, beginning with resource allocation decisions for the firm's business units? In many if not most cases, the best information choice for evaluating ongoing business-unit investments is a life-cycle track record that displays the business unit's historical performance (similar to Cummins' track record shown in Figure 2) set alongside a forecast of future life-cycle performance. The forecast's plausibility could be judged by comparison to the business unit's historical track record and to track records for competitors. Note that a lifecycle track record can be condensed into data displays that focus on economic value added (EVA).[29] One particularly valuable use of life-cycle thinking is its ability to provide milestones or guideposts, as previously discussed, as to top priorities depending upon a company's (or business unit's) life-cycle stage.

With systems thinking, the interrelatedness of the compensation plan with strategic considerations also becomes more apparent. On the one hand, the compensation plan focuses on what is measured as to financial performance and that should work to encourage long-term value creation. But at the same time, how such results are achieved is also likely to matter. This link to strategy and the means of value creation ties back to a company's degree of success in sustaining a knowledge-building culture that facilitates the training, support, and motivation of employees at all levels to be problem solvers who excel in building teamwork and collaboration.[30] An integral part of an innovative, well-functioning culture is the development and promotion of leaders with the right skills for the job. The higher one goes in the management ranks, the more important becomes their systems thinking skill.

This line of thinking is echoed by Paul Polman, former CEO of Unilever, who has a stellar track record in leading a large firm that created substantial value for stakeholders while being uniquely successful in promoting sustainability. In Polman's words,

> I truly believe that future leaders will be systems thinkers. It is inconceivable that anyone will successfully steer companies, or countries, through our volatile world without understanding the interdependencies between the systems on which we depend.[31]

The culture so described is likely to prove the bedrock of an innovation process that, when successful, shows up as favorable fade in life-cycle track records. And to promote and reinforce such a culture, the compensation plan should be long-term oriented with two well-designed and complementary components: financial performance and culture performance.

Systems thinking encourages the questioning of assumptions and soliciting of diverse views that are likely to shed light on promising solutions to specific problems or even better ways of organizing the firm and how it is managed. When the CEO and board are fully engaged with systems thinking, major changes can be expedited because of a shared goal to improve the performance of the overall system (the entire firm itself) and greater willingness to disrupt business as usual. Management and boards that cling to a business-as-usual mindset coupled with greenwashing communications about emission reductions will surely prove laggards in the new Net Zero world.

A board's fiduciary duty with respect to its company's long-term survival and prosperity requires that directors periodically evaluate their firm's past and projected future long-term financial performance. Such a viability test should include, as noted, *a comparison of returns-on-capital versus the cost of capital* and address not only a status-quo scenario of no carbon tax, but also multiple scenarios addressing a range of plausible future carbon taxes (per ton of carbon dioxide gas equivalent emitted). Such a test may well lead to large-scale changes in strategy and/or restructuring of business units.

Concluding thoughts

Too much attention to looking good on the basis of trendy ESG metrics can easily turn out to be at cross-purposes with a long-term planning horizon keyed to innovation. A sizable portion of a company's major innovations may not move the needle much in terms of ESG metrics but may score high in the eyes of customers as to value creation (and quite possibly improve their customers' ESG performance). Recent research shows a tendency during quarterly earnings conference calls for those managements who have reported weaker-than-expected profits to talk less about financial results and more about their ESG progress.[32] Keep in mind that innovation is the key to *sustainable progress* that jointly delivers on financial performance and taking care of future generations through environmental improvements.

Expect the most significant innovations that advance the Net Zero transition to be delivered by managements that question assumptions, experiment, expand their firm's knowledge base, and continually adapt their business model to a fast-changing world—resulting in high ROIs achieved on new investments.

NOTES

[1] Bartley J. Madden. 2023. "Bet on Innovation, not ESG Metrics, to Lead the Net Zero Transition." *Journal of Applied Corporate Finance*. 35: 35-44. https://doi.org/10.1111/jacf.12554. This article, in slightly modified form, was originally published as Bartley J. Madden. 2022. "Bet on Innovation, not Environmental, Social and Governance Metrics, to Lead the Net Zero Transition." *Systems Research and Behavioral Science*. 1-12. https://doi.org/10.1002/sres.2915.

[2] For especially comprehensive analyses, see the annual reports prepared by the United Nations Intergovernmental Panel on Climate Change (IPCC). For a succinct summary of the issues, see Bill Gates. 2021. *How to Avoid a Climate Disaster: The Solutions We Have and the Breakthroughs We Need.* New York: Alfred A. Knopf.

[3] Robert S. Kaplan and Karthik Ramanna. 2021. "Accounting for Climate Change." *Harvard Business Review* November-December 120–131.

[4] C. S. Holling. 2001. "Understanding the Complexity of Economic, Ecological, and Social Systems." *Ecosystems* 2001 (4): 390–405.

[5] Nizar Abdelkafi and Karl Tauscher. 2016. "Business Models for Sustainability: Sustainability From a System Dynamics Perspective." *Organization & Environment* 29 (1): 74–96.

[6] Tobias Hahn, Lutz Preuss, Jonatan Pinske, Frank Figge. 2014. "Cognitive Frames in Corporate Sustainability: Managerial Sensemaking with Paradoxical and Business Case Frames." *Academy of Management Review* 39(4): 463–487.

[7] Michael C. Jackson. 2019. *Critical Systems Thinking and the Management of Complexity.* Hoboken, NJ: John Wiley & Sons p. xix.

[8] Canan Acar and Ibrahim Dincer. 2019. "Review and evaluation of hydrogen production options for better environment." *Journal of Cleaner Production* 218: 835–849.

[9] Andrew I. Fillat and Henry I. Miller. 2021. "Nuclear Power is the Best Climate-Change Solution by Far." *Wall Street Journal* 4 November op-ed.

[10] Marco Alvera. 2021. *The Hydrogen Revolution: A Blueprint for the Future of Clean Energy.* New York: Basic Books pp. 6,7, and 167.

[11] Bartley J. Madden. 2021. "The Pragmatic Theory of the Firm." *Journal of Applied Corporate Finance* 33(1): 98–110.

[12] Martin Geissdoerfer, Paulo Savaget, Nancy M. P. Bocken, and Erik Jan Hultink. 2017. "The Circular Economy—A new sustainability paradigm?" *Journal of Cleaner Production* 143 (February) 757–768.

[13] Nigel Roome and Celine Louche. 2016. "Journeying Toward Business Models for Sustainability: A Conceptual Model Found Inside the Black Box of Organizational Transformation." *Organization & Environment* 29(1): 11–35.

[14] John D. Sterman. 2001. "System Dynamics Modeling: Tools for Learning in a Complex World." *California Management Review* 43(4): 8–25.

[15] Tobias Hahn, Jonatan Pinke, Lutz Preuss, and Frank Figge. 2015. "Tensions in Corporate Sustainability: Towards an Integrative Framework." *Journal of Business Ethics* 127(2): 297–316.

[16] David Shugar, Diana Myers, and Danielle Fugere. 2022. "Road to Zero Emissions: 55 companies ranked on Net Zero Progress." As You Sow www.asyousow.org.

[17] For a summary of leading-edge approaches to carbon capture, see Adam Vaughan, "The race to capture carbon." *New Scientist* 19 February 2022, 20–21.

[18] James F. Moore. 1993. "Predators and prey: A new ecology of competition." *Harvard Business Review* (May): 75–86.

[19] Shirley Sagawa and Eli Segal. 1999. "Common Interest, Common Good: Creative Value Through Business and Social Sector Partnerships." *California Management Review* 42(2): 105–122.

[20] Deborah Dougherty and Danielle D. Dunne. 2011. "Organizing Ecologies of Complex Innovation." *Organization Science* 22(5): 1214–1223.

[21] William D. Nordhaus. "Climate Change: The Ultimate Challenge for Economics." Nobel Prize lecture December 8, 2018.

[22] Idil Gaziulusoy, Carol Boyle, Ron McDowall. 2013. "System innovation for sustainability: a systemic double-flow scenario method for companies." *Journal of Cleaner Production* 45 (April): 104–116.

[23] Bartley J. Madden. 2020. *Value Creation Principles: The Pragmatic Theory of the Firm Begins with Purpose and Ends with Sustainable Capitalism*. Hoboken, NJ: John Wiley & Sons. Also, David A. Holland and Bryant A. Matthews. 2018. *Beyond Earnings: Applying the HOLT CFROI and Economic Profit Framework*. Hoboken, NJ: John Wiley & Sons.

[24] The inflation-adjusted cost of capital for U.S. public companies was estimated at 5.95% in Eugene F. Fama and Kenneth R. French. 1999. "The Corporate Cost of Capital and the Return on Corporate Investment." *Journal of Finance* 54(6): 1939-1967.

[25] Alan Ohnsman. 2022. "Big Green Machines." *Forbes*. February/March p. 40.

[26] Michael E. Porter, George Serafeim, and Mark R. Kramer. "Where ESG Fails." *Institutional Investor* online October 16, 2019.

[27] Mark Van Clieaf. 2020. "Designing Performance for Long-Term Value: Aligning Business Strategy, Management Structure, and Incentive Design." In Richard Leblanc (Ed.) *The Handbook of Board Governance*. 2nd edition. Hoboken, NJ: John Wiley & Sons.

[28] Michael C. Jensen and Joe Fuller. 2003. "What's A Director to Do?" In *Best Practices: Ideas and Insights from the World's Foremost Business Thinkers*. Cambridge, MA: Perseus Publishing.

[29] Bartley J. Madden. 2020. *Value Creation Principles: The Pragmatic Theory of the Firm Begins with Purpose and Ends with Sustainable Capitalism*. Hoboken, NJ: John Wiley & Sons summarizes the pros and cons of life cycle versus EVA data displays on pp. 176–177 and discusses the challenge of incorporating intangibles into financial performance metrics in Chapter 5. Also, see Mark L. Frigo and Bartley J. Madden. "Strategic Life-cycle Analysis: The Role of the CFO." *Strategic Finance* October 2020 pp. 33–39.

[30] Elliot S. Schreiber. 2021. *The Yin & Yang of Reputation Management*. London: Enlightened Enterprise Media.

[31] Paul Polman. "Tackle sustainability challenges with a systems-based approach." *International Business Times* January 20, 2014.

[32] Ryan Flugum and Matthew E. Souther. 2021. "Stakeholder Value: A Convenient Excuse for Underperforming Managers?" Working Paper. https://ssrn.com/abstract=3725828.

CHAPTER 6

The Madden Center for Value Creation at Florida Atlantic University

Mission

In the preface and overview, I discussed the research passions that fueled my work in finance and in knowledge building. That fire is still burning. However, it became time to plant seeds for the future with a value creation center at a major university. Such a center would advance three goals that are logical extensions of my life's work.

- **Promote value creation** as a foundational guiding principle to achieve widespread prosperity.
- **Contribute to a worldwide educational platform** that provides an intellectual foundation to motivate and assist young people in becoming value creators.
- **Focus academic research on the firm** as the fundamental unit of analysis for economic progress, giving particular attention to knowledge building, systems thinking, and value creation.

I had two items on my checklist for securing a home for the Madden Center for Value Creation. First, connect with a highly accomplished academic leader who has the proverbial *fire in the belly* to build a center that excels in achieving the above goals. Second, feel comfortable that the dean of the business school and I share the same beliefs about free-market capitalism and the need to provide an affordable educational opportunity for young people that enables them to rise as high as their skill and determination can take them.

Fortunately, the ideal connection was made at Florida Atlantic University (FAU) in Boca Raton, Florida, which is a little over a two-hour drive from our home in Naples. Siri Terjesen is the Phil Smith Professor of Entrepreneurship and Associate Dean of the business school. A top-notch academic, with charisma and an amazing work ethic (also raising three delightful children), she is the perfect founding Executive Director of the Madden Center for Value Creation. Dean Dan Gropper does a superb job in leading one of the largest business schools in the U.S. His educational philosophy is rooted in the primacy of a free enterprise economic system with technical business skills complemented by a broad education in the sciences and liberal arts. Michael Ryall is Professor of Management and the Center's Policy Director. He has made significant contributions to the development of the Value Capture Model that offers business strategy insights. Mark Packard is Associate Professor and the Center's Director of Research. His book, *Entrepreneurial Valuation*, provides a deep dive into the customer value experience. Susan Dennett is Instructor and Operations Director of the Center. Susan developed and is the driving force behind the Center's Certificate in Value Creation online course.

Activities

Longer-term success at the Madden Center will contribute to making the world a better place. More specifically, our work can transcend the polarization epitomized by capitalism versus socialism or Democrat versus Republican. And in so doing, we can build a more civil society rooted in building knowledge that creates value for others while ensuring that no one is left behind. Value creation is a way of thinking that cuts across political ideologies to the benefit of all.

The Madden Center hosts visiting scholars from all over the world who are conducting value-creation research. These scholars include doctoral students as well as professors and span all business fields, including management, finance, accounting, and corporate governance. Their visits last from two weeks to a year, and there have been Fulbright Scholars.

The Madden Center faculty affiliates pursue research topics related to value creation and worldwide prosperity. Topics include regulation and specifically FDA reform, higher education accountability, health care, and entrepreneurship. The Madden Center partnered with World Scientific for publication of *Value Creation, Entrepreneurship, and Public Policy* with contributions from FAU faculty members that relate to principles discussed in my *Value Creation Principles* book.

The Madden Center hosts a wide range of conferences and events. Some recent conferences include the Entrepreneurship, Longevity, and Biotech Conference, the Higher Education and Value Creation Conference, and value-creation research for special issues in the Academy of Management Perspectives. The Center also hosts events to support free speech on college campuses and offers civics training in person to incarcerated individuals in South Florida at the South Bay Correctional Facility and Moore Haven Correctional Facility.

Our Advisory Board is a diverse group of business and academic leaders, including Nobel Laureate Vernon Smith. The Madden Center was officially designated as one of only ninety university centers across the U.S. as an "Oasis of Excellence" by the prestigious Washington, DC-based American Council of Trustees and Alumni (ACTAL).

I am maximum bullish on our Certificate in Value Creation online course which takes about thirty hours of study and has seven units that expand on the ideas presented in seven chapters of my *Value Creation Principles* book. Importantly, the course consolidates articles and videos from worldwide experts that are especially relevant to the value-creation topics covered. Consolidation of this material in an easily digestible format enables participants to make connections that otherwise they would likely not make.

Each of the first two cohorts in 2023 included fifteen hundred participants from forty countries. The course will continue to evolve and improve over time. Feedback is encouraging. For example, an email from a high-level executive in India's largest bank: "The course was incredibly insightful and enriching, and I genuinely appreciate the dedication and expertise of the faculty and staff at Florida University's Madden Center. The knowledge and skills I gained during this course will undoubtedly be invaluable in my professional journey. . . . I look forward to the possibility of working together." India, and developing nations in general, hold significant potential for large-scale distribution of the online course.

The Madden Center's Certificate in Value Creation online course is on its way to earning worldwide adoption in business schools, in business firms and other organizations, and by individuals seeking a more rewarding life as a value creator.

As I am writing this chapter, conversations are ongoing about a value-creation educational platform focused on making value creation a global standard for business. The Madden Center is benefitting from insights provided by Gautam Mahajan, the founding editor of the *Journal of Creating Value*, and Hunter Hastings, the host for the *Value*

Creators podcast. The proposed platform would be an online, internet-accessible central place for many self-directed learners to gain access to well-designed courses (e.g., the Madden Center's Certificate in Value Creation Course) supplied by the core group of founding organizations. As a platform that facilitates communication and learning, assistance will be provided to business and educational leaders thinking about the startup of new value-creation centers worldwide. Echoing the spirit of this initiative, I gave the following address to the graduates of FAU College of Business:

Commencement speech at the FAU College of Business, December 16, 2021

I am honored to be asked to speak at your graduation ceremony, to share my thoughts, and be with all of you on this special day. As I have walked around the campus of this growing university, I feel the energy, the spirit, the sense of hope, and excitement about the future.

I began my career as an engineer and then served in the Army during the Vietnam War. I concluded that a career in business was right for me, and I then earned my MBA. That graduate degree opened a world of exciting possibilities for me. Your hard work in earning your graduate degree will lead to similar exciting opportunities for you to make the world a better place.

Most of my career has focused on researching the performance of business firms, the connection between long-term firm performance and market valuation, and the overriding imperative of a knowledge-building-value-creation culture.

What I have come to believe is that value creation is the foundation for a prosperous society. And, for sure, I am excited about the work that will be done by the new Madden Value Creation Center in the college of business at Florida Atlantic University.

I encourage you to commit your working careers to being value creators who continually build knowledge and strive for win-win relationships always. Value creation is about efficiently doing work that contributes to what a customer or client wants or what a patient needs. Non-value-adding work is waste. A value-creation culture is rooted in constructive skepticism about what we think we know to be true and a desire to experiment and discover root causes of problems.

I have four recommendations as to planning your long-term working careers. First, here is the key question: Will working for this organization better improve my problem-solving skills and expand my knowledge base versus alternative opportunities?

Second, be wary of working for highly bureaucratic organizations with a pyramid command-and-control organizational structure and excessive management layers. In these organizations, typically the next level down does whatever it takes to meet the accounting-based performance goals of the next level up. In this type of environment, lower-level employees are not mentored to improve their problem-solving skills. The result: work easily becomes a real grind.

Third, seek employment in organizations where the culture supports you, and where you will be mentored and have opportunities to improve your skills. Avoid organizations where people at the top think they have all the answers. Be adventurous in which industries you consider, while looking for organizations where your work could genuinely create value for customers, clients, or patients.

When you have an opportunity to talk with employees of a particular organization, ask probing questions that can reveal if the culture is one of routinely doing whatever it takes to make the accounting targets and looking for your manager to devise a work-around for significant problems that you encounter. Or is the culture one of mentoring employees to develop their problem-solving skills so that employees continually expand their knowledge base. The preferred culture will tend to be encountered in flatter organizations versus pyramid command-and-control organizations.

Fourth, you want to work at organizations that will prosper in the future and offer more opportunities for advancement. Spend time reading what the CEO says about the purpose of their organizations. For publicly traded firms, read the shareholder letters written by the CEOs, which are in the firm's annual report, and any other material you can find. This will also help for job interviews. You are looking for a knowledge-building-value-creation culture that avoids business-as-usual complacency and instead questions core assumptions, takes pride in experimentation, and adapts early to a changing world.

On my list of the best CEOs of all time are Ken Iverson of Nucor (a steel company noted for its flat organizational structure) and Brad Smith of Intuit (consumer financial software and developer of QuickBooks). Iverson noted: "We anticipate and accept that roughly half of our investments in new ideas and new technologies will yield no usable results . . . Our managers focus on shaping an environment that frees employees to determine what they can do and should do to the benefit of themselves and the business." Smith noted: "Our rapid experimentation culture cuts through hierarchy . . . creating an environment where everyone can innovate, and debate turns into doing."

These quotes are emblematic of the type of culture in which employees have the freedom to create value to the benefit of all of the organization's stakeholders.

In conclusion, let today's graduation mark the beginning of a journey to live the life of a value creator—all the while striving for win-win relationships. And, in so doing, you certainly can make the world a better place.

The Madden Center and FDA reform

BACKGROUND

A good friend of mine, Frank Burroughs, lost his daughter Abigail to neck cancer. She was valedictorian of her high school class and died just as her adult life was beginning at age twenty-one. Losing a child is a parent's worst nightmare, but Frank's loss was compounded by the haunting knowledge that Abigail's life might have been saved if only she had been prescribed a breakthrough drug, Erbitux. Abigail's highly regarded oncologist wanted to prescribe Erbitux, but he couldn't do so legally because Erbitux hadn't yet been approved by the FDA. Frank tried to get Abigail into a clinical trial, but she didn't meet the precise conditions required (as discussed later, clinical trials carefully restrict admissions). So Abigail applied for a compassionate use exemption to FDA policy but she was denied. Erbitux was eventually approved to treat exactly the type of cancer that Abigail had, but sadly, it was too late for Abigail.

Frank decided to channel his grief and devote his life to helping people who are on death's doorstep battling life-threatening diseases. He co-founded the Abigail Alliance for Better Access to Developmental Drugs to assist patients trying to gain expanded access, also called compassionate use, for promising therapeutic drugs that are (too) slowly making their way through the FDA's clinical trial process.

A few days before she died, Abigail did an extensive television interview as part of an effort by her and her father to educate people about the life-and-death consequences of the lack of patient access to promising new drugs. During the interview, Abigail told the audience, "This is not just about me. This is about many others."

The Abigail Alliance sued the FDA to try to establish a constitutional right to save one's life by accessing a not-yet-approved drug. Andrew von Eschenbach was the head of the FDA at that time, and the Abigail Alliance for Better Access to Developmental drugs vs. von

Eschenbach reached the Supreme Court. In 2008, the Supreme Court declined to hear the case.

Ironically, we learned later that Andrew von Eschenbach's heart and mind supported the Abigail Alliance! After he left his FDA Commissioner position, von Eschenbach wrote an insightful op-ed in the *Wall Street Journal*:

> Breakthrough technologies deserve a breakthrough in the way the FDA evaluates them. Take regenerative medicine. If a company can grow cells that repair the retina in a lab, patients who've been blinded by macular degeneration shouldn't have to wait years while the FDA asks the company to complete laborious clinical trials proving efficacy. Instead, after proof of concept and safety testing, the product could be approved for marketing with every eligible patient entered in a registry so the company and the FDA can establish efficacy through post-market studies.[1]

My work on improving the FDA regulatory system and bringing patients better drugs, sooner, at lower cost was inspired by Frank, Abigail, and the many patients who might have lived under a better system for approving drugs. This work evolved into a book, *Free To Choose Medicine: Better Drugs Sooner at Lower Cost,* journal articles, a monograph, countless op-eds, and participation in many video interviews.[2] While I find the intellectual argument for Free To Choose Medicine (FTCM), as explained in this chapter, to be truly compelling, the bigger motivation is to secure *freedom* for patients, advised by their doctors—using all relevant up-to-date treatment results available. They should be the ones to make informed decisions about accessing promising but not-yet-FDA-approved drugs in the context of their unique health conditions and their unique risk preferences.

FOREWORD TO THE 3RD EDITION OF FREE TO CHOOSE MEDICINE

Vernon Smith was awarded the 2002 Nobel Prize in Economic Sciences. I was honored when Vernon agreed to write the Foreword for the 3rd edition of *Free To Choose Medicine*.[3] Here's Vernon summarizing the key ideas of FTCM.

> There are two kinds of error when considering the harm that any drug testing-approval process can cause. There is the error of approving a drug that may have safety and efficacy risks, and the error of failing to approve in a timely manner a drug that can prevent deaths already occurring. The balancing of these two errors is politically difficult for the FDA. Why? Because any drug that gets through the FDA screen and causes injury or death is likely to cause widespread negative publicity for the agency and calls for tightening the FDA's already too-fine screen or otherwise "doing something" to prevent recurrence.
>
> Alternatively, any drug that is delayed for a year or two or longer and would have been efficacious will fail to prevent injury or death for those who are not treated—silent private events that are not newsworthy, but in aggregate cause large amounts of unnecessary suffering and death. This tradeoff is inherent in the uncertainties of medical treatment and the advance of knowledge. It is not due to evil people. Everybody involved can be doing his or her job faithfully according to the rules, but those rules are failing to correct a growing imbalance between the damages caused by these two types of error.
>
> . . . Using sound economic principles, [Madden] argues that the FDA's one-size-fits-all regulatory scheme is flawed. It does not allow individuals to express their preferences for risk versus potential health improvement. Moreover, there is no

feedback mechanism to evaluate the benefits versus costs of the hugely expensive and lengthy FDA clinical trials. The negative consequences to society of failing to modify this regulatory process will worsen as the pace of medical innovation accelerates. Hence, the importance of reforms in FDA procedures is overdue.

> . . . The first component of Madden's plan is a dual track arrangement. On one track, new drugs continue along the conventional FDA clinical-testing procedures. On a separate track, independent of the FDA, new drugs that have passed both Phase I safety tests and one or more Phase II clinical trials can be bought by informed consumers (patients with advice from their doctors) by legally contracting with drug developers. Patients and their doctors could choose either FDA-approved drugs or new drugs still in clinical trials. The second component is a Tradeoff Evaluation Drug Database (TEDD) that allows convenient access to the information patients and doctors need to be adequately informed about the risks of adverse side effects and potential health improvements. TEDD also incorporates the private sector in a way that promotes informed choice among alternatives throughout the system.[4]

FTCM AND THE DRUGS-TO-PATIENTS SYSTEM

It is rare to encounter a holistic analysis of the FDA's performance from the perspective of the overall drugs-to-patients system. Each stakeholder views the system only through their own constricted lens. So, for example, biopharmaceutical companies view it as a business; patients as something they need when sick; and regulators as something to control. And politicians have multiple views: potential voter blame for allowing the FDA to approve a drug that unexpectedly kills people, a source of campaign contributions from drug developers, and an opportunity to make the world a better place (for patients). While none of these perspectives are wrong, none captures how the whole system works. Applying systems thinking to the drugs-to-patients system reveals both the opportunity for FTCM to significantly improve how patients can gain early access to promising drugs and the weakness of the arguments of FTCM critics.

The FDA's stated regulatory purpose is to provide safe and effective drugs (biologics, medical devices, etc.). However, let's focus on what people want. We want to live longer, healthier, and productive lives. Therefore, we want better drugs, sooner, at lower cost. Let's take a look at what the FDA regulatory system delivers.

We see a regulatory system that, for successful drugs, takes drug developers a dozen years or so to pass through clinical testing and the approval process, and, including the cost of failed drugs, a tab exceeding $2 billion to secure a single approval. That produces sky-high prescription drug prices and an invisible graveyard of patients who died while potential life-saving treatments were laboriously moving through the clinical testing process.

In my work, I emphasize the role of language in hiding assumptions. "Safe" and "effective" are relative terms that depend upon the individual patient's unique health situation and unique risk preferences. As Vernon Smith highlighted earlier, the FDA does not have access to that information. Consequently, it approves or denies based on its view of the "average" patient using statistical processes. This does make their job easier as to approval decisions but fails to deal with the wide diversity of unique patient situations. A new drug (alone or in combination) that barely misses statistical significance in clinical testing as a stand-alone treatment may produce strikingly effective treatment results for a subset of patients.

FDA proponents claim that it uses the gold standard for clinical testing—Randomized Control Trials (RCTs)—whereby a control group gets a placebo and the other group gets the real deal. There is a serious ethical issue with giving a placebo to a control group of seriously ill patients. Moreover, the FDA is extremely stringent in allowing patients to enter a clinical trial (recall Abagail's inability to secure a spot). For statistical purposes, the FDA wants a homogeneous population for a clinical trial. Ideally, all of the patients are in good health except for having the medical problem under investigation. The FDA's goal and process meet its needs but not those for whom early access to the most promising new and not-yet-FDA-approved drugs could be life-changing or lifesaving.

We see the advantages of a dual track arrangement in which the status quo FDA clinical testing process represents one track and the other "free to choose" track offers much-needed competition for the status quo. Here's how the free to choose track works: After successful completion of Phase I safety trials and one or more Phase II safety/efficacy trials, a drug developer could request conditional FDA approval for, say, two years. This can be renewed for up to eight years depending upon treatment results. At any time, based on demonstrated patient benefits, the FDA could confer full approval; otherwise, at the end of eight years, the conditional approval expires. Keep in mind that treatment results clearly inferior to approved drugs lead to loss of conditional approval. Treatment results are real-world data as opposed to RCT data. FTCM is a voluntary self-adjusting system attuned to our needs for better drugs, sooner, at lower cost.

ENABLING A SELF-ADJUSTING SYSTEM

Patients' genetic data, biomarkers, etc. and treatment results could be posted in a Tradeoff Evaluation Drug Database (TEDD). This registry could yield three huge benefits:

- Doctors and patients see up-to-date treatment results for all patients who have voluntarily chosen to use the drug.

- Doctors could compare their patient's genetic data, biomarkers, etc. to similar subgroups on the FTCM track. Strikingly good or bad treatment results for these subgroups would guide doctor/patient decisions. Importantly, subgroups could evolve to include the conditional approval drug in combination with one or more approved drugs far more quickly than conventional RCTs.
- At the level of the overall drugs-to-patients system, we see that FTCM benefits the biopharmaceutical industry by boosting R&D effectiveness and startup biotech firms by boosting the supply of capital.

TEDD provides a gold mine of real-world data (especially subgroup data) that would lead to both quicker and improved R&D decisions by the biopharmaceutical industry that, in turn, would lead to a large-scale boost in innovation. In addition, put yourself in the position of venture capitalists who analyze potential investments in both biotech startups and other startups that don't involve a decade or more waiting for a potential FDA approval. A nascent biotech firm with leading-edge scientists but little capital might have a revolutionary approach to cure cancer, Alzheimer's, and the like. However, waiting a decade or more while the startup tries to navigate future capital-raising events while hopefully advancing its science is typically viewed unfavorably by venture capitalists. Moreover, a clinical trial may fail to reach the FDA's statistical milestones but yield subgroups that deliver superb results. In addition, the causal mechanism as to why subgroups performed as they did is now understood. Good luck, says the FDA. Hindsight bias doesn't count, so go raise funds for a new clinical trial and the three years it typically takes to run a clinical trial.

What happens to a biotech firm with a radically different approach to developing a potential cure for a serious disease when it enters the

Phase III clinical trial, which is the pivotal last trial before the FDA renders an approval decision? The FDA will impose very difficult-to-achieve endpoints for the trial because the firm's approach does not conform to approved drugs coupled to the FDA's unrelenting fear of negative publicity due to a mistaken approval decision. Of course, this makes a potential breakthrough even more risky in the eyes of venture capitalists. They are keenly aware of how the startup biotech world is fraught with problems and delays, all the while eroding a hoped for above-average return on their invested capital.

Contrast the above scenario with FTCM, wherein if the science works so that Phase I safety and Phase II safety/efficacy are successful, conditional approval can lead to revenues in three years or less. In the eyes of venture capitalists, the FTCM environment is enormously more attractive vs. the status quo. This would cause a sustained upsurge of high-risk capital to fund biotech startups, thereby scaling up innovation.

What about the "gold standard" RCTs? If time and money were not considered, I agree that RCTs are the preferred approach to evaluate new drugs. However, FTCM with early access coupled to real world data monitoring is especially needed for patients dealing with life-threatening medical conditions. With FTCM, patients can access innovative new drugs up to five to seven years earlier compared to the status quo.

The self-adjusting mechanism of FTCM is straightforward and a win-win for all, including the FDA with its concerns for monitoring safety and efficacy. Patients, advised by their doctors, can stick with FDA-approved treatments or voluntarily chose a conditional-approval drug. These are informed decisions using TEDD data. If TEDD reveals unsatisfactory treatment results, usage plummets, and vice versa. This decentralized transmission of information is how a market system should work to the benefit of all as emphasized by Friedrich Hayek.

Importantly, TEDD would track subgroups (genetic data, biomarkers, etc.) of patients. Certain subgroups could do much better or much worse than the average treatment outcome. This is uniquely valuable information for patients (and their doctors) who can then determine whether or not the patients fit particular subgroups. Note that, compared to the excruciating slow pace of RCT information flow, TEDD provides up-to-date, critically important information at a super-fast pace.

FDA CULTURE

Why doesn't the FDA jump on the idea of bringing better drugs to market, sooner, at lower cost? One can understand an organization's (public or private) actions and performance by putting under the microscope its culture, which in turn, is nurtured and sustained by its leadership. For the FDA, its commissioner is equivalent to a private sector CEO. My time spent analyzing FDA behavior and studying the pro and con academic literature about the FDA is summarized in the following three characteristics of FDA culture:

- Promote a public perception that the FDA's processes are essential in order to provide safe and effective drugs.
- Protect the FDA's monopoly power to grant access to new drugs. (Squash any competitive threat such as FTCM.)
- Avoid negative publicity from FDA-approved drugs that subsequently generate unexpectedly high mortality or terrible side effects. (The result is a relentlessly increasing demand for ever more expensive and time-consuming clinical testing.)

Needless to say, FDA commissioners embrace this culture; it comes with the job. Remember Andrew von Eschenbach didn't fully embrace FDA reform, at least not publicly, until he was no longer commissioner! To be clear, this isn't a criticism of von Eschenbach but simply recognizing that culture and incentives constrain the FDA. FTCM strikes at the heart of FDA culture, which, in turn, is an anchor preventing structural change needed for the FDA to deliver superior performance in a fast-changing environment.

The faster the pace of medical innovations, the more beneficial early access via FTCM becomes to patients. Who can deny the likely rapid generation of future health-changing medical innovations that include a deeper understanding of biological cause and effect, enhanced biometrics, gene therapy and editing, stem cells, bioprinting of human organs, nanoparticles for imaging plus drug and gene delivery, and artificial intelligence, to name just a few?

The FDA's purpose-driven culture is to provide safe and effective drugs. But I'll argue that a far more useful purpose is better drugs, sooner, at lower cost. Realistically however, in the near term, replacing the FDA's purpose of safe and effective drugs is certainly a bridge too far for FTCM supporters.

CRITICISM AND REPLY

I have studied many FDA criticisms of proposals to reform the FDA. These are crafted by obviously highly intelligent FDA employees. The points they make logically fit together although in a myopic way programmed to defend the FDA culture. However, their logic crumbles with two points that are rarely addressed in their criticisms:

1. The FDA's purpose should be better drugs, sooner, at lower cost.
2. With advances in big data analytics and artificial intelligence coupled to an especially fast pace of medical innovations, RCTs should no longer be viewed as a gold standard. Real-world data can be effectively utilized to deliver better drugs sooner for seriously ill patients.

The government of Japan is deeply concerned about the development and availability of innovative treatments for its aging population—a concern that should be shared by many other nations. According to the policy brief "Free To Choose Medicine in Japan: A Model for America":

> Masaru Uchiyama, president of Japanese for Tax Reform, explained that he heavily promoted a 2007 Japanese translation of an early version of Madden's FTCM book "to government ministries and agencies, pharmaceutical companies, medical equipment manufacturers, [nongovernment organizations] critical to government policy, pharmacodynamics litigation organizations, etc." He observed local government officials offered support for this approach at parliamentary study meetings.
>
> The influence of Madden's FTCM plan is evident from some of the criticisms of the Free To Choose Model.[5]

Uchiyama's promotion of FTCM was instrumental in Japan's passage of legislation implementing some FTCM principles for regenerative medicine treatments (i.e., treatments not suited to RCTs, such as stem cells). Regrettably, Japan did not implement the feedback database TEDD described earlier. In 2019, the prestigious journal *Science* published "Downgrading of regulation in regenerative medicine" by Douglas Sipp and Margaret Sleeboom-Faulkner. They implied that I had zero interest in benefitting humankind and that I even (fasten your seat belt) did the following: "The author of FTCM has since thanked the translator [Masaru Uchiyama] for helping to make his ideas into law in Japan."

My reply to the *Science* article was published in 2020 in *Econ Journal Watch*, in which I point out that my critics make judgments that are not substantiated by evidence or argumentation. My reply covered many of the key points discussed in this chapter and need not be repeated. However, there were two additional points in the article.

First, RCTs are viewed by FDA proponents as the gold standard, implying an absence of negative unintended consequences. This is patently false. For example, since cancer survival rates (a key RCT readout) are far less costly to measure for late-stage cancer patients compared to early-stage cancer patients, all else equal, this incentivizes drug developers to allocate resources to late-stage cancer drugs.

And second, FDA proponents typically assert that FTCM would impair drug safety. On the contrary, safety advocates should support FTCM. Recall that RCTs strive for a homogeneous patient population in a trial. Note that FTCM involves a heterogenous population far more likely to reveal adverse side effects. Also, an effective conditional approval drug that gains increasing usage would almost certainly have been used by a far greater number of patients vs. limited RCT populations. Consequently, a successful conditional approval drug would almost certainly have more robust safety assessments than RCT drugs.

THE PROMISING PATHWAY ACT AND THE CRITICAL ISSUE OF MARKET PRICING

In mid-2023, with bipartisan support, the Promising Pathway Act (PPA) was introduced in the Senate and the House. Senator Mike Braun (R-Indiana) was instrumental in making this happen, as were two of my friends—Al Musella, founder of the *Musella Foundation for Brain Tumor Research & Information*, and Keith Desserich, co-founder of *The Cure Starts Now*. It would implement FTCM principles for seriously ill patients. The PPA is ideally suited to the anticipated rapid pace of medical innovations in the twenty-first century. And, if passed, it would add much-needed competition for the status quo.

As this legislation progresses, what might be the FDA's reaction?

Well, based on the three characteristics of FDA culture, bet on strong opposition. FDA proponents will draw a line in the sand where they stand for safe and effective drugs. They also will drum up fear that any weakening of FDA powers would eventually unleash a torrent of harmful drugs on the public.

FDA proponents imply patients and doctors are not smart enough to access TEDD data and make informed decisions that are in their best interests. They will point out that expanded access (compassionate use) via FDA regulation and Right to Try federal legislation signed by President Trump in 2018 already provide fast access to those on death's doorstep. However, both options do not scale for the same fundamental reason: drug developers have no economic incentive to participate. Legally, distribution of a not-yet-approved drug requires the drug developer to sell the drug, which can be in limited supply, to patients at cost. And use of the drug by patients on death's doorstep will be associated with patient deaths. Moreover, compassionate access assumes drug developers will divert their attention from the hoped-for FDA approvals needed for their survival.

It is critically important for the PPA to allow for market pricing. As such, drug developers are incentivized to price their conditional approval drugs at favorable prices to patients (and insurance companies) in order to gain increased usage and generate real world data demonstrating patient benefits and warranting full FDA approval.

Right to Try became a powerful rallying call and garnered widespread popular support at the state level, where forty-one bills were signed into law. The Promising Pathway Act may well gain similar popular support, enabling informed medical decisions that are in our best interests. Keep in mind that the federal Right to Try legislation, signed by President Trump in 2018, failed to allow for market pricing and failed to live up to expectations.

Sure, let's keep the existing system in place but add a free to choose track that works for patients in desperate need and disseminates information quickly to those who need it the most. We can all put our shoulder to the freedom wheel and convince our politicians to enthusiastically support and pass the Promising Pathway Act. As Abigail said, this is not just about me.

Dean Dan Gropper, me, and Siri Terjesen, the Founding Executive Director of the Madden Center for Value Creation. Florida Atlantic University, business school commencement, December 16, 2021.

NOTES

[1] Andrew von Eschenbach. "Medical Innovation: How the U.S. Can Retain Its Lead." *Wall Street Journal.* February 14, 2012. https://www.wsj.com/articles/SB10001424052970203646004577215403399350874.

[2] Op-eds are available at: http://learningwhatworks.com. I did a two-part interview with PBS TV. Part 1: https://www.youtube.com/watch?v=fq650Mm_q6E. Part 2: https://www.youtube.com/watch?v=e1L_URVwHL0. Progress Potential, and Possibilities: https://www.youtube.com/watch?v=Y2AwJ7_ci3A.

Consumer Choice Center: https://www.youtube.com/watch?v=uvVx0VQxp3A.

[3] For a particularly insightful book review, see: http://learningwhatworks.com/papers/FTCM%20book%20review%20IJPEE.pdf.

[4] Bartley J. Madden. 3rd ed. 2018. *Free To Choose Medicine: Better Drugs Sooner at Lower Cost.* Arlington Heights, IL: Heartland Institute.

[5] Edward Hudgins. June 2018. "Free To Choose Medicine in Japan: A Model for America." Policy Brief. Heartland Institute. https://heartland.org/publications/free-to-choose-medicine-in-japan-a-model-for-america/.

Epilogue

The Bartley J. Madden Foundation

Looking to the future, I expect investments that I have made in privately held, early-stage firms to fund a significant acceleration in the activities of the Bartley J. Madden Foundation. The mission of our family foundation is to promote value-creation principles as the foundation for a prosperous society. Prosperity is more widely shared through a society rooted in dynamism with enthusiastic support for experimentation, knowledge building, and innovation by firms, and especially by entrepreneurial startups.

We support:

- Programs that focus on teaching value-creation skills, which can include online platforms and on-the-job mentoring and, in general, helping people gain opportunities for earned success.
- Initiatives to improve our educational system, including expanded school choice, that realistically can improve performance in delivering value to customers (parents and students).
- Initiatives to instill private sector innovation and efficiency into government processes.
- Programs that nurture and sustain free speech, especially on college campuses.
- Programs to assist veterans of our armed services to transition to productive lives in the private sector.
- Research with the potential to deliver practical insights about coordinating knowledge-building proficiency and organizational

structure to upgrade the long-term performance of organizations in both the private and public sectors.

- Public policy research focused on innovative approaches to legislation and regulation that embrace systems thinking, competition, and adaptation in a fast-changing world.

Family

In looking to the future, including our planned revving up of the Madden Foundation, I keenly appreciate the role of my family in so many ways. For example, in 2022, I received a "simple" epidural injection to reduce pain in my neck. That led to a massive amount of infected blood throughout my spine. Multiple complex surgeries saved my life. When your family members are there every step of the way, it tends to focus the mind on what is important in life.

I'll provide a brief snapshot of my sons, daughters, and wife. My oldest son, Gregory, is a lawyer and earned his Juris Doctorate from Northern Illinois University. For many years, he managed a team at the Department of Veterans Affairs National Acquisition Center primarily concerned with large contracts for biopharmaceutical products. He currently is co-chair of the Coalition for Government Procurements Healthcare Pharmaceutical subcommittee. Greg joined the ranks of entrepreneurs after his stint with government work and started Orlaithe Consulting. Greg's firm has been exceptionally successful in guiding large firms through the complexities of government contracts. Greg is President of the Madden Foundation and no one is better equipped to fill this leadership role. Greg and his wife, Peg, put enormous energy into raising two daughters, Sarah and Katie, both straight A students who excel at theater (Sarah) and sports (Katie).

My younger son, Jeffrey, earned his degree in business from the University of Iowa followed by a highly successful twenty-year career in money management. He became a partner at Ironbridge Capital Management and later Senior Vice President at RMB Capital. Jeff developed a special expertise in analyzing biopharmaceutical companies. In 2021, he received a money manager of the year award for the exceptional risk-adjusted returns, over multiple time periods, earned by his small/mid-cap stock fund. Currently, Jeff is a co-founder and CEO of ADvantage Therapeutics, a company that is advancing a novel immunotherapy (fast tracked in the U.K.) for Alzheimer's in a Phase IIb clinical trial and doing pioneering work on the Klotho protein that has unique properties to slow the aging process. Jeff orchestrated the acquisition of Klogenix, which enabled Dr. Carmela Abraham—a world-class Alzheimer's and Klotho scientist—to become Chief Scientific Officer of ADvanatage. The result is a firm at the forefront of redefining approaches not only for combatting Alzheimer's but also for the aging process.

My older daughter, Miranda, received her degree in law enforcement from Western University in Illinois. And because of her interest in health care, she shifted gears and earned a CNA (certified nursing assistant) certification. Currently, she works in the corporate office at Edwards Hospital in Naperville. Miranda is a perfectionist in organizing information and getting jobs done—the type of person you want on your team. Her longer-term plan is to move to Florida and earn a master's degree in health administration at Florida Gulf Coast University, not far from where Maricela and I live.

Our younger daughter, Lucinda, earned her degree in art education from Illinois State University. She is a middle school art teacher in Naperville. Lucy has a unique talent for connecting with younger people. Other teachers continually seek insights from her as to how she is able to get troubled kids to change their behavior in her classroom. Lucy plans to follow her sister and move to Florida in order to earn a master's degree in social work at Florida Gulf Coast University.

My wife, Maricela, grew up in a Mexican family in which everyone contributed by working at an early age. Maricela once bought a house for her parents that realistically she could not afford. To handle the mortgage payments, she worked two full-time jobs—selling jewelry in a retail store and as a waitress at night in a sports bar. This went on for two years and reflects her values and commitment to family. We click. My research productivity jumped into high gear after I married her. I became a happy workaholic, eagerly spending time with her and all my kids when I am not grinding out the research work. Maricela earned her degree in art history from North Central College, which is located in Naperville, Illinois, near a Victorian house where we lived for ten years. We spent four years restoring the A. A. Smith house, which was built for the first president of North Central College in the 1870s. (Our family story about living in the house is posted on the internet, "The A. A. Smith House.") Maricela handled the interior and exterior design, landscaping, and procurement of an endless quantity of late nineteenth-century hardware and furniture. A photograph at the end of this chapter shows Maricela and me the first time we met our adopted daughters in a hotel room in Guatemala. My life is fundamentally a partnership with Maricela and so, too, with raising our daughters. It is a gross understatement to say that Miranda and Lucinda are close to their mom or that I love Maricela.

I proposed, Maricela said yes, and this photo was immediately taken, 1994.

I am holding Miranda, and Maricela is holding Lucinda. First time we met our soon-to-be-adopted daughters in Guatemala, 1997.

Family photo, Naperville, Illinois, 2004. Left to right, Miranda, Jeff, me, Maricela, Lucinda, and Greg.

My younger son, Jeff, after he reached the summit of Mont Blanc (Alps).

My older son, Greg, with his wife, Peg, in 2011. Their younger daughter, Katie, is on the left, and Sarah is on the right.

Maricela and me on our 27th anniversary, June 3, 2022.

Printed in France by Amazon
Brétigny-sur-Orge, FR

32820633R10127